PUBLISHER'S NOTE

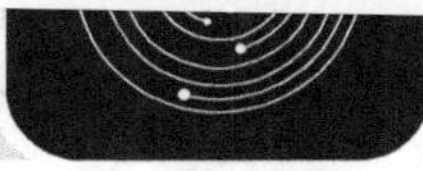

V&S Publishers has carved a significant niche in the publishing industry over the last decade, having successfully published more than 1000 titles across 9 languages spanning over 50 subject categories. Being known for the quality of content, we have built a reputation of excellence and reliability. We have consistently delivered **"Value & Substance"** to our readers, through a wide range of titles across a variety of genres covering school books, fiction and non-fiction that caters to different people from every section of the society.

The **Olympiad Guidebooks for classes 1-10** across all subjects, launched almost a decade ago, under the **GEN X Imprint**, became a go-to-source for the school students in no time, owing to their invaluable and substantive content written in a guidebook pattern,.

Having successfully sold a million copies of the same and in response to demand by both students as well as shopkeepers nationwide; we now present before you our newly launched **Olympiad Workbook Series**, designed for **classes 1-10 across 4 subjects**.

The workbooks are meticulously curated by a team of experienced educators, researchers and subject matter experts, edited by professionals and peer reviewed by teachers. The team has poured its efforts and expertise into creating a crisp and concise workbook which will help and guide the students to the path of success in Olympiad exams. The **MCQs** identified will not only help in scoring top marks in Olympiads but also inculcate a sense of deeper understanding of the subject, by way of solving **HOTS** and referring to complete solutions at the end of the book.

Here we present our new release– **OLYMPIAD WORKBOOK (NCO) CLASS–1** having following features:

- ☞ Based on the latest syllabi
- ☞ MCQs with comprehensive coverage of topics
- ☞ HOTS Questions liberally included
- ☞ A dedicated chapter on logical reasoning
- ☞ Model test paper for thorough practice
- ☞ Sample OMR sheet for real time simulation

We have made sure through our best efforts, that this workbook strictly follows the latest syllabi and patterns of the Olympiad Examination.

As **V&S Publishers** continuously strive to enhance the readability and maintain the credibility of our academic publications, we seek the support of our valuable readers in influencing and enriching the lives of future generations of students.

P.S. While every care has been taken to ensure the correctness of the content, if you come across any error, howsoever minor, do not hesitate to discuss with teachers while pointing that out to us in no uncertain terms.

We wish you all the best for your exams!

DISTINCTIVE FEATURES

01 Learning Objectives

They list the whole chapter as subtopics, helping the teachers to guide children in a step-by-step manner.

02 Multiple Choice Questions

MCQs act as an excellent learning aid, helping you to understand and work on your mistakes.

03 HOTS (Achievers Section)

The High Order Thinking Questions aim to help the student to solve Application-based questions and gain practical understanding of the subject.

04 Model Test Paper

Model test paper are provided at the end of each book, which help the student to test the knowledge which they have gained after thorough reading of all chapters.

05 Answer Key

Detailed Answer Key along with explanations aid the pupil to indentify, understand the mistakes they make during the course of Olympiad preparation.

NCO

OLYMPIAD WORKBOOK

1

NATIONAL CYBER OLYMPIAD

- **01** Learning Objectives
- **02** Multiple Choice Questions
- **03** HOTS (Achievers Section)
- **04** Model Test Paper
- **05** Answer Keys and Solutions
- **06** OMR Answer Sheet

V&S PUBLISHERS

Published by:

V&S PUBLISHERS

F-2/16, Ansari road, Daryaganj, New Delhi-110002
☎ 23240026, 23240027 • *Fax:* 011-23240028
✉ info@vspublishers.com • ⊕ www.vspublishers.com

Online Brandstore: amazon.in/vspublishers

Regional Office : Hyderabad
5-1-707/1, Brij Bhawan (Beside Central Bank of India Lane)
Bank Street, Koti, Hyderabad - 500 095
☎ 040-24737290
✉ vspublishershyd@gmail.com

Follow us on:   

BUY OUR BOOKS FROM: AMAZON   FLIPKART

DISCLAIMER

While every attempt has been made to provide accurate and timely information in this book, neither the author nor the publisher assumes any responsibility for errors, unintended omissions or commissions detected therein. The author and publisher makes no representation or warranty with respect to the comprehensiveness or completeness of the contents provided.

All matters included have been simplified under professional guidance for general information only, without any warranty for applicability on an individual. Any mention of an organization or a website in the book, by way of citation or as a source of additional information, doesn't imply the endorsement of the content either by the author or the publisher. It is possible that websites cited may have changed or removed between the time of editing and publishing the book.

Results from using the expert opinion in this book will be totally dependent on individual circumstances and factors beyond the control of the author and the publisher.

It makes sense to elicit advice from well informed sources before implementing the ideas given in the book. The reader assumes full responsibility for the consequences arising out from reading this book.

For proper guidance, it is advisable to read the book under the watchful eyes of parents/guardian. The buyer of this book assumes all responsibility for the use of given materials and information.

The copyright of the entire content of this book rests with the author/publisher. Any infringement/transmission of the cover design, text or illustrations, in any form, by any means, by any entity will invite legal action and be responsible for consequences thereon.

CONTENTS

INTRODUCTION TO COMPUTER

LEARNING OBJECTIVES

➤ Basics of Computer

MULTIPLE CHOICE QUESTIONS

1. Which of the following is NOT a man-made machine?

(A)  (B) 

(C)  (D) 

2. Which of the following tasks a computer can do for you?
   (A) Drink water (B) Eat food
   (C) Play music (D) All of these

3. Identify the following:
   - It is an electronic machine that never gets tired.
   - You can play songs on it.

(A)  (B) 

(C) 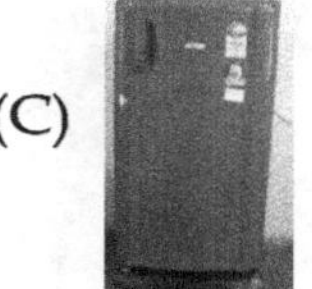 (D) 

4. Which of the following runs on electricity?

(A) 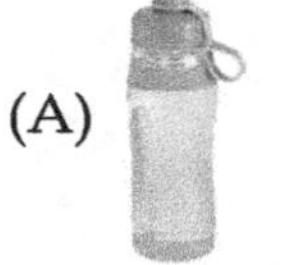 (B) 

(C)  (D) 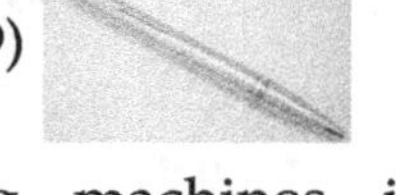

5. Arrange the following machines in largest to smallest order, according to the amount of space they take on a table.

1. 

2. 

3.

(A) $1 \to 2 \to 3$ (B) $2 \to 3 \to 1$
(C) $3 \to 2 \to 1$ (D) $1 \to 3 \to 2$

6. Which of the following types of computers can be used to play games?

(A)    (B) 

(C)    (D) All of these

7. With the help of given type of machine, you can ___________ .

(A) Listen to music
(B) Stitch clothes
(C) Build House
(D) Plant trees

8. Which of the following is NOT a type of a computer?
(A) Laptop   (B) Tablet
(C) Palmtop   (D) Tabletop

9. Select the CORRECT match.

(A) 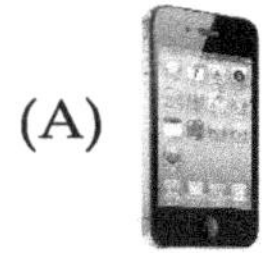   – Mobile Phone

(B)    – Laptop

(C)    – Tablet computer

(D)    – Desktop computer

10. Which of the following is/are man-made and electronic machines?

1.    2.    3. 

(A) Only (1)
(B) Only (2)
(C) Only (3)
(D) All (1), (2) and (3)

11. What is a device?
(A) It is a machine designed for a particular purpose.
(B) It a natural thing made by nature.
(C) It is an artificial thing made by nature.
(D) All of these

12. Select the CORRECT statement about the jumbled letters given below.
CMOUPETR
(A) It is a man-made machine.
(B) It is not an electronic machine.
(C) You cannot play music on it.
(D) You cannot solve sums on it.

13. Which of the following machines help you in your homework like solving sums?

(A) 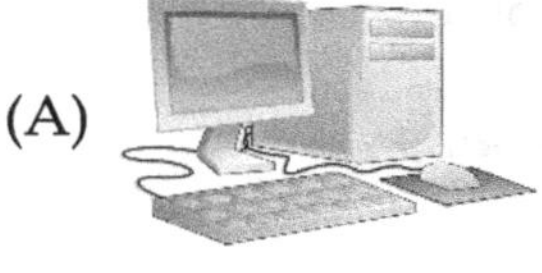

(B) 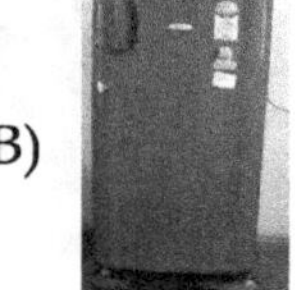

(C)

(D) Both (A) and (B)

14. Identify the pictures given below:

Now, which of the following words would it form, by using the first letter of these pictures?

(A) LAPTOP

(B) TABLET

(C) PATLET

(D) BATLET

15. How many machine names are hidden in the given grid?

M	E	H	R	A	Y	T	H
N	A	V	N	E	E	T	M
C	O	M	P	U	T	E	R
Z	G	I	S	W	P	N	Y

(A) 1   (B) 3

(C) 4   (D) 2

HOTS (ACHIEVERS SECTION)

16. Which of the following statements is CORRECT about the given device?

(A) It is a type of computer.

(B) It can be carried from one place to another.

(C) It is called laptop.

(D) All of these

17. Identify the pictures marked as 1 and 2 and select the CORRECT statement.

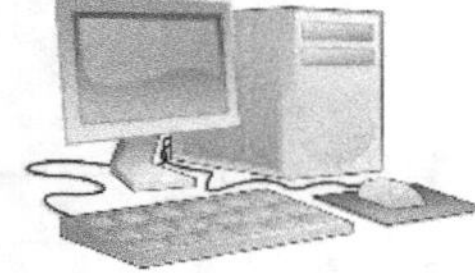

1   2

(A) 1 – It is a man-made machine and it runs on fuel.

  2 – It is an electronic machine.

(B) 1 – It is made by nature.

  2 – It is not a man-made machine.

(C) 1 – It is not a man-made machine

  2 – It is an electronic machine.

(D) 1 – It is an electronic machine.

  2 – It is made by nature.

18. Anu wants to do the following tasks:

– Watch movies

– Play songs

– Play games

Which of the following devices can she use?

(A) 

(B) 

(C) 

(D) All of these

19. Match the following.

Column-1	Column-2
(A)	1. It can be carried in a pocket easily.
(B)	2. It can easily fit onto your lap.
(C)	3. It needs a table where you can place this machine.

(A) (a) – 2, (b) – 3, (c) – 1
(B) (a) – 1, (b) – 2, (c) – 3
(C) (a) – 2, (b) – 1, (c) – 3
(D) (a) – 1, (b) – 3, (c) – 2

20. Computer is known as a smart machine because __________ .
(A) It does not make mistake on its own.
(B) It never gets tired.
(C) It works very fast.
(D) All of these

1.	Ⓐ Ⓑ Ⓒ Ⓓ	5.	Ⓐ Ⓑ Ⓒ Ⓓ	9.	Ⓐ Ⓑ Ⓒ Ⓓ	13.	Ⓐ Ⓑ Ⓒ Ⓓ	17.	Ⓐ Ⓑ Ⓒ Ⓓ
2.	Ⓐ Ⓑ Ⓒ Ⓓ	6.	Ⓐ Ⓑ Ⓒ Ⓓ	10.	Ⓐ Ⓑ Ⓒ Ⓓ	14.	Ⓐ Ⓑ Ⓒ Ⓓ	18.	Ⓐ Ⓑ Ⓒ Ⓓ
3.	Ⓐ Ⓑ Ⓒ Ⓓ	7.	Ⓐ Ⓑ Ⓒ Ⓓ	11.	Ⓐ Ⓑ Ⓒ Ⓓ	15.	Ⓐ Ⓑ Ⓒ Ⓓ	19.	Ⓐ Ⓑ Ⓒ Ⓓ
4.	Ⓐ Ⓑ Ⓒ Ⓓ	8.	Ⓐ Ⓑ Ⓒ Ⓓ	12.	Ⓐ Ⓑ Ⓒ Ⓓ	16.	Ⓐ Ⓑ Ⓒ Ⓓ	20.	Ⓐ Ⓑ Ⓒ Ⓓ

PARTS OF COMPUTER

2

➤ Main Parts of Computer

MULTIPLE CHOICE QUESTIONS

1. Which of the following is NOT a part of a computer?

(A) 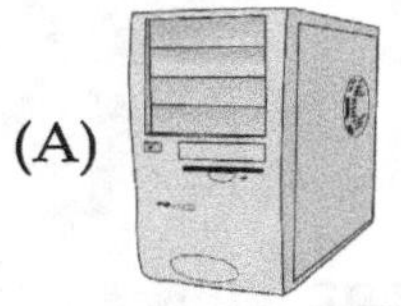

(B) 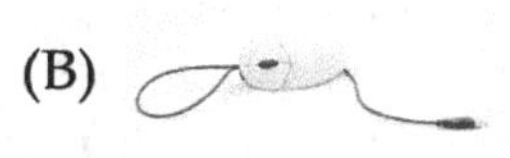

(C) 

(D) 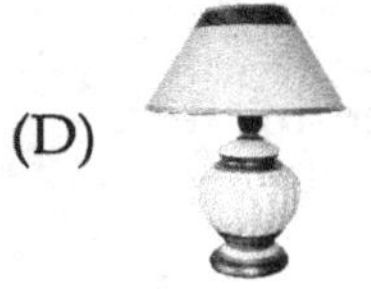

2. Which of the following parts of a computer is used to watch movies?

(A) 

(B) 

(C) 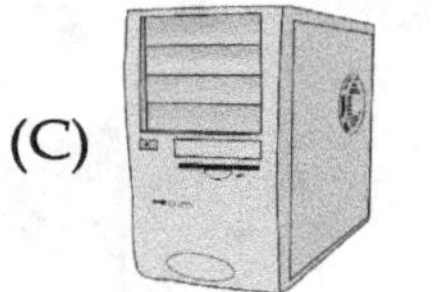

(D)

3. Which of the following parts of a computer can be connected wirelessly?

(A) 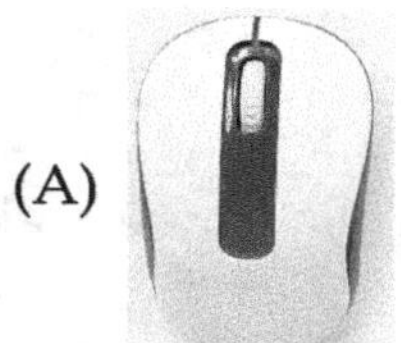

(B) 

(C) 

(D) Both (a) and (b)

4. Select the INCORRECT match.

(A) 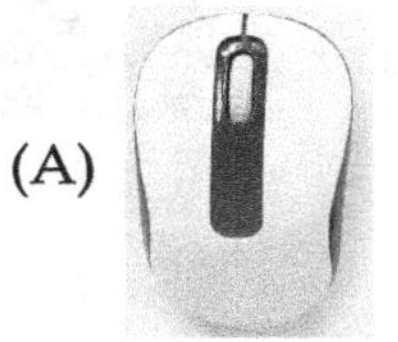 – Printer

(B)  – Keyboard

(C)    – Speakers

(D) 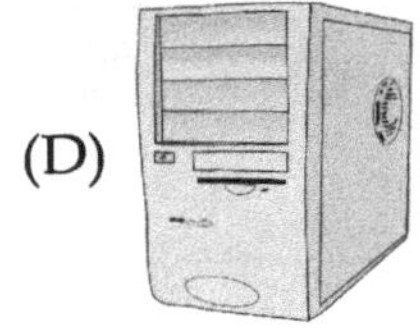   – CPU

5. The given device is called __________. It is used to enter __________ into the computer.

(A) Mouse, letters and symbols
(B) Keyboard, letters and symbols
(C) Printer, Photos
(D) Speakers, Photos

6. Which of the following parts of a computer can be controlled by the given device?

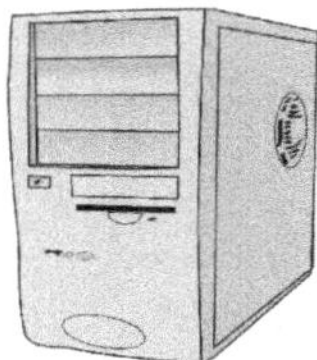

(A) Mouse   (B) Keyboard
(C) Monitor   (D) All of these

7. Which of the following devices is needed if you want to listen songs on a computer?

(A)    (B) 

(C) 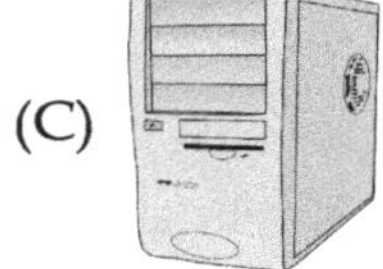   (D) 

8. Which of the following devices is used to point and select items on computer screen?

(A)    (B) 

(C) 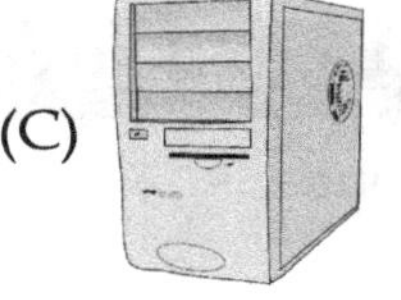   (D) 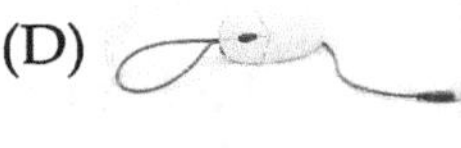

9. You want to do the following tasks:
   - To type letters in a computer.
   - To create a copy of those letters onto the sheet of paper.

Which of the following parts of computer is/are needed?
(A) Keyboard
(B) Printer
(C) Speakers
(D) Both (a) and (b)

10. Which of the following statements is CORRECT about the given part of a computer?

(A) It is known as printer.
(B) It is used to take photos.
(C) It is used to listen songs.
(D) None of these

11. __________ is the basic part of a computer which controls the overall working of a computer.

(A)    (B) 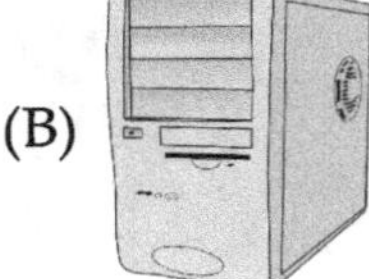

(C)

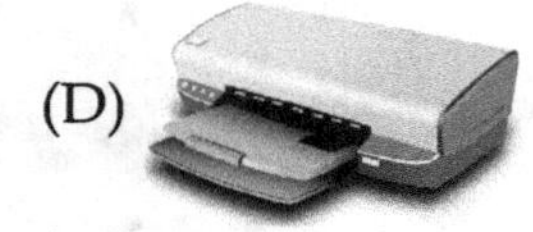

(D)

12. Select the odd one out (regarding parts of a computer).

(A)

(B)

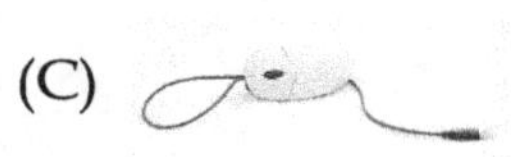

(C)

(D)

13. Which of the following parts of computer copies information from the computer screen on a sheet of paper?

(A)

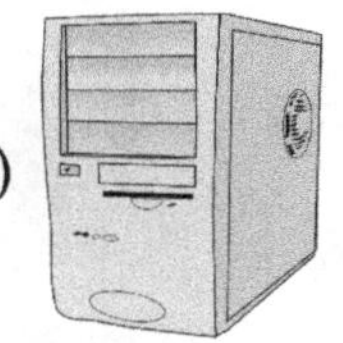

(B)

(C)

(D)

14. Identify the picture for the given jumbled letters.

MNOIRTO

(A)

(B)

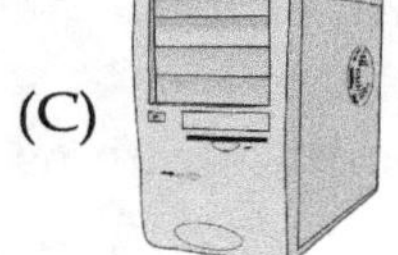

(C)

(D)

15. Whatever you type on keyboard is shown on __________ .

   (A) Monitor   (B) Mouse
   (C) CPU   (D) Printer

16. Identify the parts of computer marked as 1 and 2 and select the CORRECT statement.

1.

2.

(A) 1 – It is used to listen recorded sound.
    2 – It is known as speakers.
(B) 1 – It is known as speakers.
    2 – It is known as monitor.
(C) 1 – It is used to type letters.
    2 – It is used to point items on computer.
(D) Both (A) and (B)

17. How many parts of a computer are hidden in the grid shown here?

M	O	U	S	E	Y
C	P	U	T	W	X
Z	H	V	T	H	A

(A) 1   (B) 2
(C) 3   (D) 4

18. Identify the following:
- It can be wirelessly connected to the computer.
- It is used to enter letters and numbers into the computer.

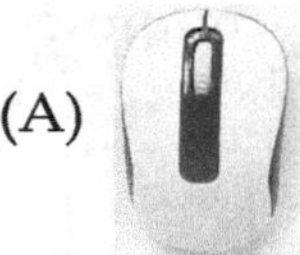

(A)

(B)

(C)

(D)

19. Select the CORRECT statement about the given jumbled letters.

MUOES

(A) It is used for pointing items on computer screen.
(B) It is used to enter letters on computer.
(C) It is used to listen to music.
(D) It controls all the working of computer.

20. Match the following:

Column-1   **Column-2**

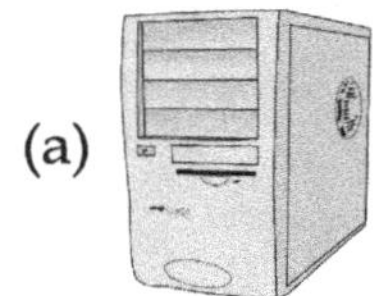

(a)

1. Used to watch movies

(b)

2. Known as brain of a computer

(c)

3. Used to type letters into the computer

(A) (a) – 2, (b) – 3, (c) – 1
(B) (a) – 1, (b) – 2, (c) – 3
(C) (a) – 2, (b) – 1, (c) – 3
(D) (a) – 1, (b) – 3, (c) – 2

HOTS (ACHIEVERS SECTION)

21. Mr. Sinha has a DVD of a new movie. He wants to watch this movie. Is it possible for him to watch the movie on the computer?

(A) Yes
(B) No
(C) Possibility is less
(D) Possibility is more

22. How many parts of a computer are hidden in the grid shown here?

M	O	U	S	E	Y
C	P	U	T	W	X
Z	H	V	T	H	A

(A) 1   (B) 2
(C) 3   (D) 4

23. Identify the following:

- It can be wirelessly connected to the computer.
- It is used to enter letters and numbers into the computer.

(A) 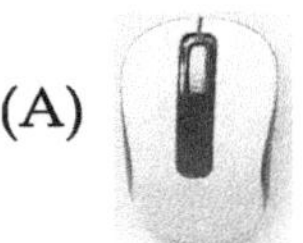

(B) 

(C) 

(D) 

24. Select the CORRECT statement about the given jumbled word.

MUOES

(A) It is used for pointing items on computer screen.
(B) It is used to enter letters on computer.
(C) It is used to listen to music.
(D) It controls all the working of computer.

25. Match the following:

Column-I		Column-II	
a	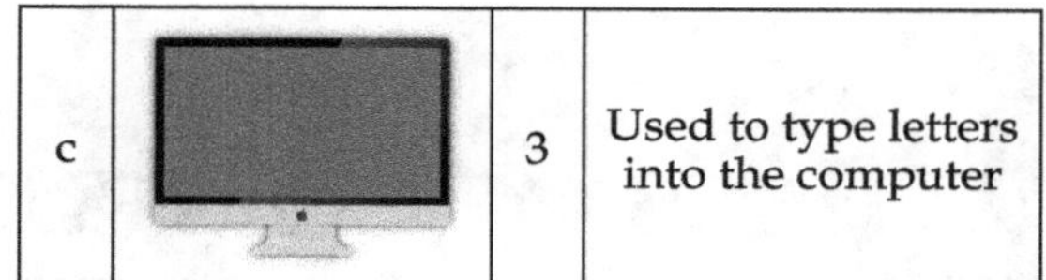	1	Used to watch movies
b		2	Known as brain of a computer
c		3	Used to type letters into the computer

(A) a-2,   b-3,   c-1

(B) a-1,   b-2,   c-3

(C) a-2,   b-1,   c-3

(D) a-1,   b-3,   c-2

USES OF COMPUTER

LEARNING OBJECTIVES

- ➤ Computers at Schools
- ➤ Computers at Homes
- ➤ Computers at Offices
- ➤ Computers at Hospitals

MULTIPLE CHOICE QUESTIONS

1. Which of the following pictures does not show the use of a computer?

   (A) 

   (B) 

   (C) 

   (D) 

2. Which of the following tasks of a TV can be performed by a computer?
   (A) Playing movies
   (B) Playing music

   (C) Managing volume
   (D) All of these

3. Select the INCORRECT statement.
   (A) Songs can be played using a computer.
   (B) A computer can be used to solve sums.
   (C) We use pencil and paper to draw on a computer.
   (D) We can play games on a computer.

4. In hospitals, computers are used to __________.
   (A) Store data about patients
   (B) To sell tickets
   (C) To record TV shows
   (D) To monitor flight timings

5. Which of the following games can be played on a computer?
   (A) Racing
   (B) Cricket
   (C) Basketball
   (D) All of these

6. Which of the following is done on a computer for fun?
   (A) Solving sums
   (B) Selling tickets

(C) Playing games

(D) Both (A) and (B)

7. Solving the sums on computers is _______.

(A) Easy and time-consuming

(B) Difficult and time-consuming

(C) Easy and fast

(D) Difficult and fast

8. Mohit, a pilot says that a computer helps him to _______.

(A) Play outdoor games on plane

(B) Send and receive games

(C) Control and monitor the flight

(D) All of these

9. Which of the following can be prepared using computers in schools?

(A) Time-Table

(B) Circulars

(C) Students Report

(D) All of these

10. We type _______ on computers.

(A) Drawings

(B) Letters

(C) Games

(D) All of these

11. Computers in homes cannot be used for _______.

(A) Typing

(B) Watching movies

(C) Playing games

(D) Updating passbooks

12. In which of the following institutions are computers NOT used for education?

(A) Schools

(B) Colleges

(C) Homes

(D) Banks

13. Which of the following types of computers can be used while travelling?

1.

2.

3.

(A) Only 1

(B) Only 2

(C) Only 3

(D) Both 1 and 3

14. With the help of computer, you can _______.

(A) Take print out

(B) Search for information

(C) Book tickets

(D) All of these

15. We watch _______ on a computer.

(A) Cartoons

(B) Movies

(C) Music

(D) Both (A) and (B)

16. Find the number of activities which can be done on a computer, hidden in the given grid.
    (A) 1   (B) 3
    (C) 5   (D) 7

V	A	X	U	S	D	E	R
D	P	L	A	Y	I	N	G
R	C	V	T	H	F	S	C
A	S	A	Y	M	R	V	B
W	O	F	P	I	C	E	R
I	T	B	I	F	I	K	L
N	O	A	N	N	K	A	N
G	N	L	G	A	T	I	O

17. Select the INCORRECT match regarding the uses of computer.
    (A) Offices – Maintaining employee records
    (B) Schools – Diagnosing diseases
    (C) Banks – Money withdrawal through ATM
    (D) Railways – Booking Tickets

18. Select the word which when unscrambled gives the name of a place where computers are used.
    (A) SMUS   (B) VOLSE
    (C) NABK   (D) POME

19. Which of the following statements is INCORRECT?
    (A) Cover of books is designed using computers.
    (B) Newspapers are printed with the help of computers.
    (C) Computers are used for making building layouts.
    (D) At departmental stores, computers are used for making toys.

20. Which of the following figures shows the correct way of drawing pictures in computer?

(A) 

(B) 

(C) 

(D) 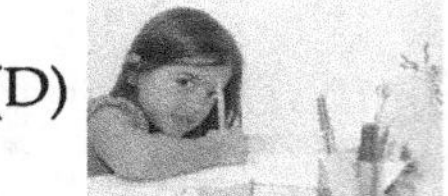

1.	A B C D	5.	A B C D	9.	A B C D	13.	A B C D	17.	A B C D
2.	A B C D	6.	A B C D	10.	A B C D	14.	A B C D	18.	A B C D
3.	A B C D	7.	A B C D	11.	A B C D	15.	A B C D	19.	A B C D
4.	A B C D	8.	A B C D	12.	A B C D	16.	A B C D	20.	A B C D

KEYBOARD AND ITS KEYS

LEARNING OBJECTIVES

➤ Number Keys   ➤ Special Keys   ➤ Arrow Keys
➤ Alphabet Keys   ➤ Space Bar Key

MULTIPLE CHOICE QUESTIONS

1. To type on a computer screen, we need a __________ .
   (A) Pencil   (B) Pen
   (C) Printer   (D) Keyboard

2. The buttons present on a keyboard are called __________ .
   (A) Wheels   (B) Keys
   (C) Scrolls   (D) Printers

3. Words and sentences are typed using __________ keys.
   (A) Number   (B) Special
   (C) Alphabet   (D) Control

4. Which of the following is NOT an alphabet key?
   (A) N   (B) M
   (C) A   (D))0

5. Whatever is typed on keyboard can be seen on the __________ .
   (A) Mouse   (B) CPU
   (C) Speaker   (D) Monitor

6. Select the INCORRECT match.
   (A) ↑ – Moves the cursor up
   (B) ↓ – Moves the cursor down
   (C) ← – Moves the cursor to left
   (D) Shift ⇧ – Moves the cursor right

7. To type capital letters, turn on the __________ key on the keyboard.
   (A) Delete   (B) Enter
   (C) Caps Lock   (D) Arrow

8. Which key can be used to type a letter in capital when Caps Lock key is OFF?
   (A) Delete   (B) Enter
   (C) Shift   (D) Arrow

9. __________ key is also called as return key.
   (A) Space bar   (B) Enter
   (C) Delete   (D) Backspace

10. Which of the following words cannot be completed with the given set of keys?
    E   A   P   H   O   F   C

(A) S _ I _T
(B) C A _ SL _ _ K
(C) S _ A C _ B _ R
(D) D E _ E _ E

11. Which of the following keys would you use to type your name and age?
(A) Number keys
(B) Alphabet keys
(C) Arrow keys
(D) Both (A) and (B)

12. _______ is the longest key on a keyboard.
(A) Delete
(B) Shift
(C) Enter
(D) Space bar

13. _______ key erases anything typed on the right of the cursor.

(A) Toggle
(B) Delete
(C) Backspace
(D) Arrow

14. Caps Lock is also called as _______ key.
(A) Toggle
(B) Return
(C) Symbol
(D) Extra

15. The keys from 0 to 9 are called _______ keys.
(A) Alphabet
(B) Arrow
(C) Number
(D) Special

HOTS (ACHIEVERS SECTION)

16. Observe the position of the cursor in the given snapshot.

RIG | HT

Cursor

Re-arrange the steps given below to replace letter R with letter T.

(1) Press | T | key

(2) Press | ← | key two times

(3) Press | Backspace | key

(A) (1)-(2)-(3)   (B) (2)-(1)-(3)
(C) (1)-(3)-(2)   (D) (2)-(3)-(1)

17. Look at the given image of keyboard. The key which will replace NM is _______ key.

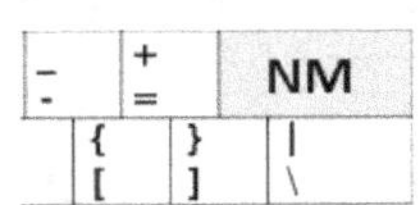

− .	+ =	NM
{ [	}]	| \

(A) Space bar
(B) Caps Lock
(C) Backspace
(D) Delete

18. What is the difference between Delete and Backspace key?
(A) Delete key is used to erase character, backspace key is used to give a small gap between two characters.
(B) Delete key erases character to the right of the cursor. Backspace key erases character to the left of the cursor.
(C) Delete key erases character to the left of cursor. Backspace key erases characters to the right of the cursor.
(D) All of these

19. Search and count the type of keys hidden in the given grid.
   (A) 5   (B) 4
   (C) 3   (D) 2

U	N	I	L	O	P	F	D	S	X
N	O	L	A	D	E	L	E	T	E
R	B	T	I	K	S	L	E	W	V
A	L	W	N	U	M	B	E	R	T
Z	B	A	C	K	B	E	T	P	A
T	A	L	P	H	A	B	E	T	R
R	V	S	M	D	G	A	I	E	D

20. Which of the following statements is INCORRECT about alphabet keys?
   (A) They are used for typing letters and words.
   (B) There are 26 alphabet keys on the keyboard.
   (C) The first six letters of alphabet keys form the name of a keyboard layout.
   (D) The last seven letters of the alphabet keys form the name of the inventor of keyboard.

1.	Ⓐ Ⓑ Ⓒ Ⓓ	5.	Ⓐ Ⓑ Ⓒ Ⓓ	9.	Ⓐ Ⓑ Ⓒ Ⓓ	13.	Ⓐ Ⓑ Ⓒ Ⓓ	17.	Ⓐ Ⓑ Ⓒ Ⓓ
2.	Ⓐ Ⓑ Ⓒ Ⓓ	6.	Ⓐ Ⓑ Ⓒ Ⓓ	10.	Ⓐ Ⓑ Ⓒ Ⓓ	14.	Ⓐ Ⓑ Ⓒ Ⓓ	18.	Ⓐ Ⓑ Ⓒ Ⓓ
3.	Ⓐ Ⓑ Ⓒ Ⓓ	7.	Ⓐ Ⓑ Ⓒ Ⓓ	11.	Ⓐ Ⓑ Ⓒ Ⓓ	15.	Ⓐ Ⓑ Ⓒ Ⓓ	19.	Ⓐ Ⓑ Ⓒ Ⓓ
4.	Ⓐ Ⓑ Ⓒ Ⓓ	8.	Ⓐ Ⓑ Ⓒ Ⓓ	12.	Ⓐ Ⓑ Ⓒ Ⓓ	16.	Ⓐ Ⓑ Ⓒ Ⓓ	20.	Ⓐ Ⓑ Ⓒ Ⓓ

COMPUTER MOUSE

LEARNING OBJECTIVES

➤ Types of Mouse

MULTIPLE CHOICE QUESTIONS

1. A computer mouse is used for __________.
   (A) Drawing pictures
   (B) Playing games
   (C) Selecting items
   (D) All of these

2. Clicking means to __________.
   (A) Press and release the left mouse button
   (B) Move the scroll wheel
   (C) Move the mouse left and right
   (D) Scroll the right mouse button twice

3. With which part of computer the tail of mouse is attached?

   (A) 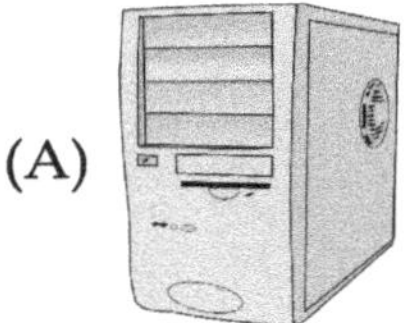 (B) 

   (C)  (D) 

4. A mouse has a wheel in the centre which is called a __________ wheel.
   (A) Track   (B) Touch
   (C) Scroll   (D) Roll

5. What does the arrow on the computer monitor shown in the given image is called?

   (A) Mouse pointer   (B) Mouse spot
   (C) Mouse track   (D) Mouse pad

6. Which finger is placed on the left mouse button?
   (A) Middle   (B) Index
   (C) Little   (D) Thumb

7. __________ clicking the mouse opens an item on computer.
   (A) Single   (B) Double
   (C) Triple   (D) None of these

8. Which of the following provides a smooth surface to move the mouse?
   (A) Monitor   (B) Mouse Pad
   (C) Mouse Cover   (D) Mouse tail

9. A mouse has __________ buttons.
   (A) 2   (B) 5
   (C) 100   (D) 150

10. Which of the following mouse actions displays a list of commands on the screen?
   (A) Right-click
   (B) Drag and drop
   (C) Scrolling
   (D) Left-click

11. Which of the following statements is CORRECT about mouse?
   (A) It is hand-operated device.
   (B) It sits outside the computer case.
   (C) It comes in many shapes and sizes.
   (D) All of these

12. A wireless mouse ___________.
   (A) Connects with the computer with a cable
   (B) Does not have a cable
   (C) Is not required to click
   (D) Is tough to operate

13. Which of the following actions is being performed in the given image?

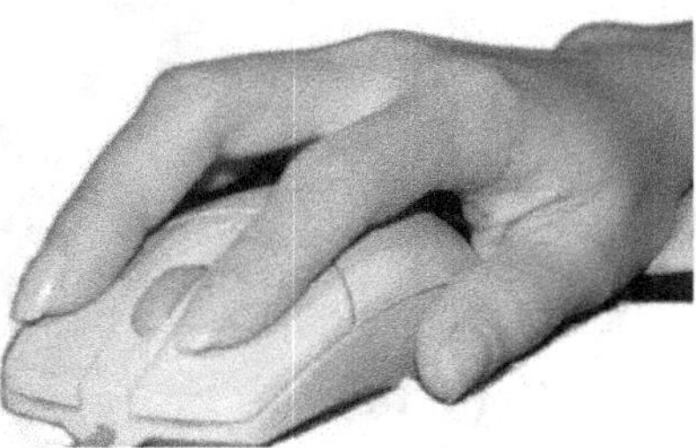

   (A) Scrolling
   (B) Wiggling
   (C) Clicking
   (D) Both (A) and (B)

14. Match the following.

Column-1	Column-2
(a) Click and drag	1. Pressing and holding the mouse button and moving
(b) Double-click	2. Moving the mouse wheel up or down
(c) Scrolling	3. Pressing the mouse button twice

   (A) (a) – (1), (b) – (2), (c) – (3)
   (B) (a) – (3), (b) – (2), (c) – (1)
   (C) (a) – (2), (b) – (3), (c) – (1)
   (D) (a) – (1), (b) – (3), (c) – (2)

15. You will see the menu as shown in the given image when you _____ the mouse.

   (A) Drag
   (B) Wiggle
   (C) Double-click
   (D) Right-click

HOTS (ACHIEVERS SECTION)

16. Unscramble the words and select the one which completes the following sentence.

   A computer mouse helps us to move the __________ from one place to another.

   (A) ROTNIMO
   (B) RINTRPE
   (B) SOUME
   (D) ROPITNE

17. Count the number of words related to mouse, which are hidden in the given grid.

T	W	I	G	G	L	E
A	S	L	M	O	R	M
N	X	C	L	I	C	K
S	F	I	T	W	R	A
M	S	C	R	O	L	L
I	P	A	C	K	B	U
R	T	T	O	N	T	A

(A) 5   (B) 4
(C) 3   (D) 6

18. Which of the following statements is CORRECT regarding mouse?

(1) Small finger is placed on the left mouse button.

(2) A mouse is always kept on rough surface.

(3) It is used for moving items on screen.

(A) Only (1)
(B) Only (2)
(C) Only (3)
(D) All (1), (2) and (3)

19. Given below is a list of action. Select which relate(s) to computer mouse?

(1) It eats grains.

(2) It helps to draw.

(3) It is controlled by hand.

(A) Only (1)
(B) Only (2)
(C) Only (3)
(D) Both (2) and (3)

20. Label the part of mouse marked by numbers (1), (2), (3) and (4).

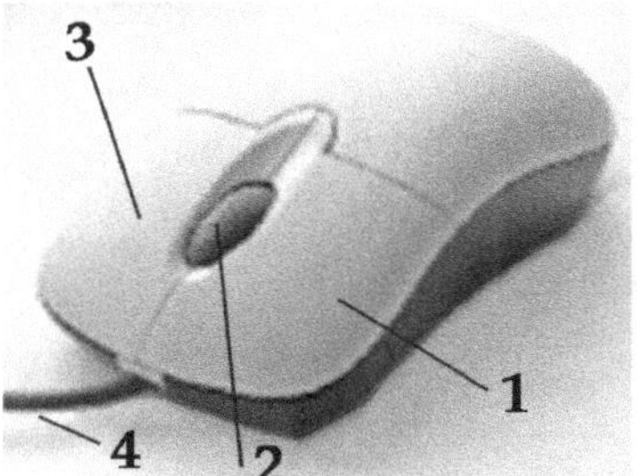

	(1)	(2)	(3)	(4)
(A)	Tail	Wheel	Left button	Right button
(B)	Left button	Wheel	Right button	Tail
(C)	Right button	Left button	Wheel	Tail
(D)	Left button	Centre button	Right button	Wheel

<hr>

1.	Ⓐ Ⓑ Ⓒ Ⓓ	5.	Ⓐ Ⓑ Ⓒ Ⓓ	9.	Ⓐ Ⓑ Ⓒ Ⓓ	13.	Ⓐ Ⓑ Ⓒ Ⓓ	17.	Ⓐ Ⓑ Ⓒ Ⓓ
2.	Ⓐ Ⓑ Ⓒ Ⓓ	6.	Ⓐ Ⓑ Ⓒ Ⓓ	10.	Ⓐ Ⓑ Ⓒ Ⓓ	14.	Ⓐ Ⓑ Ⓒ Ⓓ	18.	Ⓐ Ⓑ Ⓒ Ⓓ
3.	Ⓐ Ⓑ Ⓒ Ⓓ	7.	Ⓐ Ⓑ Ⓒ Ⓓ	11.	Ⓐ Ⓑ Ⓒ Ⓓ	15.	Ⓐ Ⓑ Ⓒ Ⓓ	19.	Ⓐ Ⓑ Ⓒ Ⓓ
4.	Ⓐ Ⓑ Ⓒ Ⓓ	8.	Ⓐ Ⓑ Ⓒ Ⓓ	12.	Ⓐ Ⓑ Ⓒ Ⓓ	16.	Ⓐ Ⓑ Ⓒ Ⓓ	20.	Ⓐ Ⓑ Ⓒ Ⓓ

STARTING AND SHUTTING DOWN A COMPUTER

LEARNING OBJECTIVES

➤ Starting a Computer
➤ Shutting down a Computer

MULTIPLE CHOICE QUESTIONS

1. The first step to start a computer is to ______.

   (A) Switch on the main power button
   (B) Press the power button on UPS
   (C) Press the power button on CPU
   (D) Switch on the monitor

2. Once the computer is on, a screen is displayed, which is called __________.

   (A) Window
   (B) Desktop
   (C) Menu
   (D) Wallpaper

3. Which of the following portions of start menu will you click to shut down the computer?

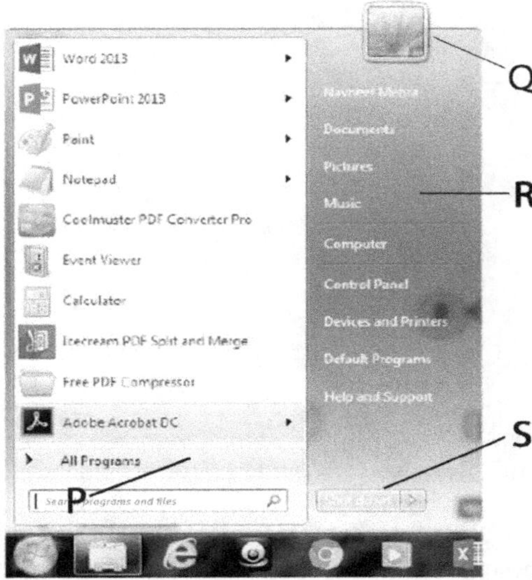

   (A) P   (B) Q
   (C) R   (D) S

"

4. After switching on the CPU, which part of computer is powered on?

(A)  (B) 

(C)  (D) 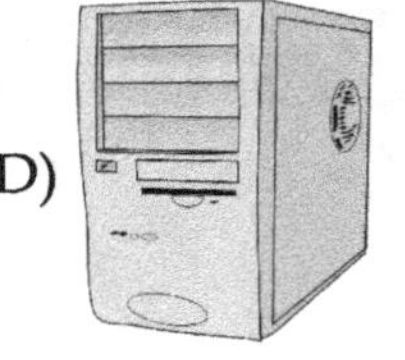

5. With the help of which part of a computer, the shut down option is selected in the start menu?

(A) 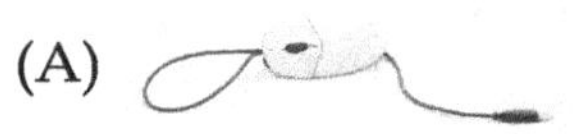 (B) 

(C)  (D) 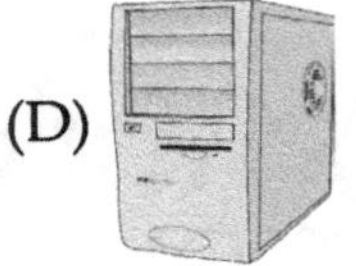

6. While working on a computer, _______.
   (A) Sit too close to the monitor
   (B) Keep the eatables away from it
   (C) Do not use the keyboard gently
   (D) Play with wires attached to computer

7. Which of the following parts is used to keep the computer on, when there is a power failure?
   (A) Monitor   (B) Keyboard
   (C) Mouse   (D) UPS

8. Which of the following options safely shuts down the computer and then starts it again?
   (A) Log off   (B) Shutdown
   (C) Restart   (D) Sleep

9. The small pictures marked as N in the given image that we see on desktop are called _______.

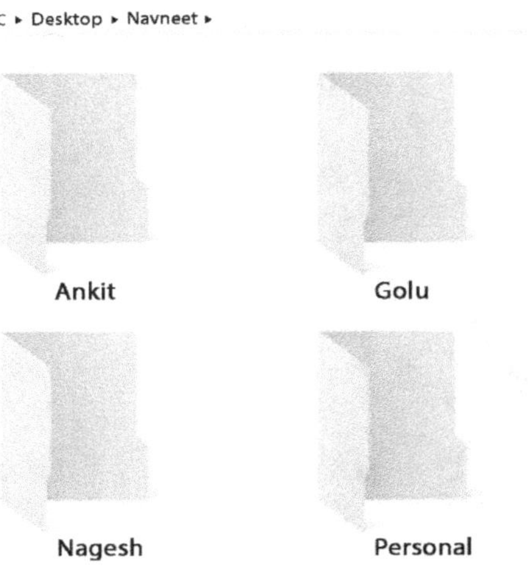
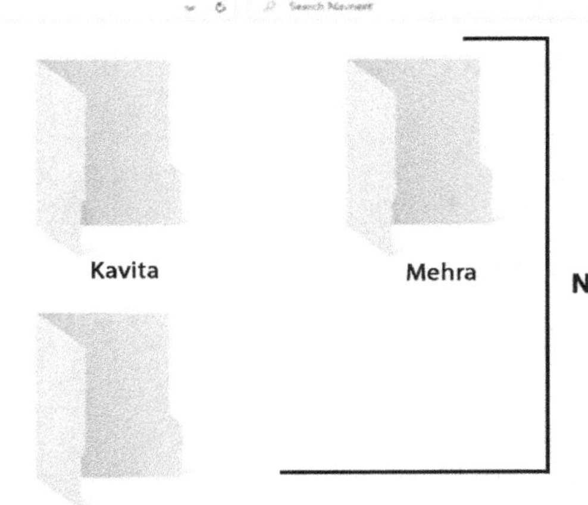

   (A) Icons   (B) Pins
   (C) Snaps   (D) Clips

10. When a computer is not in use _______.
   (A) It must be covered properly.
   (B) It must be cleaned with a wet cloth.
   (C) Its wires can be detached.
   (D) We can play with its parts.

OLYMPIAD WORKBOOK (NCO) CLASS — 1

11. How can you keep your computer dust free?
    (A) By washing it with water
    (B) By blowing air on it
    (C) By cleaning it with a dry cloth
    (D) Both (a) and (b)

12. The sequence of actions done by the computer to get everything ready for use, while starting is called _______.
    (A) Tapping   (B) Logging
    (C) Booting   (D) Clicking

13. To start a laptop, you just need to _____.
    (A) Press power button available on the laptop
    (B) Press the [🪟] key
    (C) Tap twice on touchpad

(D) Press the  key

14. A computer is switched off, when it is not in use to _________.
    (A) Supply power to its parts
    (B) Save electricity
    (C) Keep it warm
    (D) Increase its speed

15. Unscramble the given word and select the statement which is CORRECT about it.
    BOOIGNT
    (A) It is performed when computer is switched off.
    (B) It is the first step performed to start a computer.
    (C) It is performed when computer starts.
    (D) It is last step performed to shut down a computer.

HOTS (ACHIEVERS SECTION)

16. Arrange the given steps in correct order to start a computer.
    1. Switch on the CPU
    2. Switch on the monitor
    3. Switch on the UPS
    4. Switch on the power switch
    (A) (1) → (2) → (3) → (4)
    (B) (2) → (4) → (3) → (1)
    (C) (4) → (3) → (1) → (2)
    (D) (3) → (4) → (2) → (1)

17. After shutting down the computer, what is the next step to perform?
    (A) Click on the Start button
    (B) Switch off the UPS
    (C) Switch off the CPU
    (D) Switch off the Monitor

18. Unscramble the words given in Column 1 and match them with the words given in Column 2.

Column-1	Column-2
(a) GOINL	(1) End access to a computer system
(b) WODARPSS	(2) Gaining access to use computer
(c) TOGUOL	(3) Secret combination of letters and numbers

    (A) (a) – (1), (b) – (2), (c) – (3)
    (B) (a) – (2), (b) – (3), (c) – (1)
    (C) (a) – (3), (b) – (1), (c) – (2)
    (D) (a) – (3), (b) – (2), (c) – (1)

19. We use _________ and _________ to get access to the computer.
    (A) Username, password
    (B) Password, web name
    (C) Web name, crossword
    (D) Crossword, last name

20. The image given here shows the _______ step which is performed, when we start a computer.

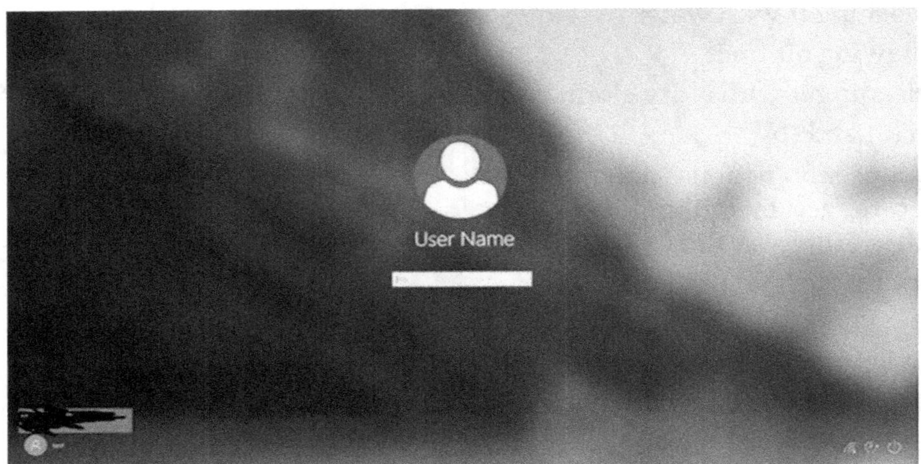

(A) First
(B) Second
(C) Last
(D) None of these

1.	Ⓐ Ⓑ Ⓒ Ⓓ	5.	Ⓐ Ⓑ Ⓒ Ⓓ	9.	Ⓐ Ⓑ Ⓒ Ⓓ	13.	Ⓐ Ⓑ Ⓒ Ⓓ	17.	Ⓐ Ⓑ Ⓒ Ⓓ
2.	Ⓐ Ⓑ Ⓒ Ⓓ	6.	Ⓐ Ⓑ Ⓒ Ⓓ	10.	Ⓐ Ⓑ Ⓒ Ⓓ	14.	Ⓐ Ⓑ Ⓒ Ⓓ	18.	Ⓐ Ⓑ Ⓒ Ⓓ
3.	Ⓐ Ⓑ Ⓒ Ⓓ	7.	Ⓐ Ⓑ Ⓒ Ⓓ	11.	Ⓐ Ⓑ Ⓒ Ⓓ	15.	Ⓐ Ⓑ Ⓒ Ⓓ	19.	Ⓐ Ⓑ Ⓒ Ⓓ
4.	Ⓐ Ⓑ Ⓒ Ⓓ	8.	Ⓐ Ⓑ Ⓒ Ⓓ	12.	Ⓐ Ⓑ Ⓒ Ⓓ	16.	Ⓐ Ⓑ Ⓒ Ⓓ	20.	Ⓐ Ⓑ Ⓒ Ⓓ

OLYMPIAD WORKBOOK (NCO) CLASS— 1

INTRODUCTION TO MS-PAINT 

LEARNING OBJECTIVES

➤ MS-Paint

MULTIPLE CHOICE QUESTIONS

1. Arrange the given steps in the CORRECT order to open MS-Paint program on your computer.
   1. Click on Start button
   2. Select Programs
   3. Click on Paint option
   4. Click on Accessories
   (A) 1 → 2 → 4 → 3   (B) 2 → 1 → 3 → 4
   (C) 2 → 4 → 3 → 1   (D) 4 → 1 → 2 → 3

2. Which of the following tools has been used in the given image?

   (A) ✏   (B) **A**
   (C) 🔍   (D) ▱

3. Which of the following tools will erase the Picture 1, to make it look like as shown in Picture 2?

Picture 1

Picture 2

4. Which of the following tools is used in drawing the given shape?

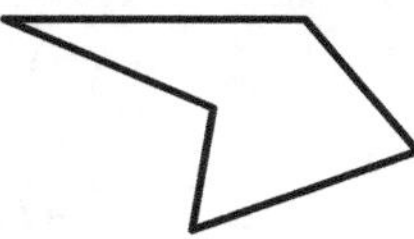

   (A) ⇩   (B) ▱
   (C) ◇   (D) None of these

5. Select the CORRECT match.
   (A) ▱ – It is used to draw free hand drawing.
   (B) □ – It is used to draw circles.
   (C) ╲ – It is used to draw straight lines.
   (D) ○ – It is used to draw rectangle.

6. Which of the following tools is NOT used while drawing the given picture?

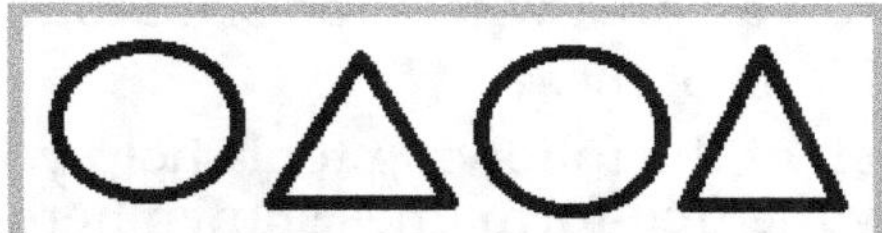

   (A) Oval tool   (B) Rectangle tool
   (C) Pencil tool   (D) Line tool

7. Which of the following tools is found in the Ribbon area?

(A)  [pencil icon]

(B) [magnifier icon]

(C)  **A**

(D) All of these

8. What is the use of the given tool?

[fill/bucket tool icon]

(A) It is used to fill the picture with colour.
(B) It is used to erase your drawing.
(C) It is used to draw shapes.
(D) All of these

9. Which of the following tools fills the given shapes with colours?

[shapes: rectangle, triangle, callout, speech bubble]

(A)  [fill tool icon]

(B)  [pencil icon]

(C)  [eraser icon]

(D)  **A**

10. Which of the following tools is NOT used to draw shapes?

(A)  [fill tool icon]

(B) [rectangle icon]

(C)  [line icon]

(D) [oval icon]

11. What is drawing area?
(A) It is an area where you can draw shapes and pictures.
(B) It is an area where you can choose colours and shapes for the drawing.
(C) It is an area where tools are found.
(D) None of these

12. Which of the following tools help you to draw the free-form lines shown here?

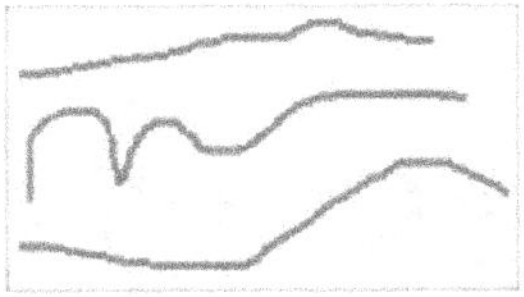

[free-form lines image]

(A)  [pencil icon]

(B)  [line icon]

(C)  **A**

(D) Both (A) and (B)

13. The given set of tools and shapes are found in ___________ .

[set of shape icons: triangle, diamond, pentagon, oval, arrows, star shapes, speech bubbles]

(A) Drawing Area
(B) Workspace Area
(C) Ribbon
(D) All of these

14. Which of the following shapes can be drawn with Line tool?

(A) [┌ shape]

(B) [└ shape]

(C)  [N shape]

(D) All of these

15. Which of the following tools is used to draw the closed shapes?

(A) [hexagon icon]

(B)  [arrow icon]

(C)  [eraser icon]

(D) Both (A) and (B)

16. Which of the following tools is NOT used in drawing the given picture?

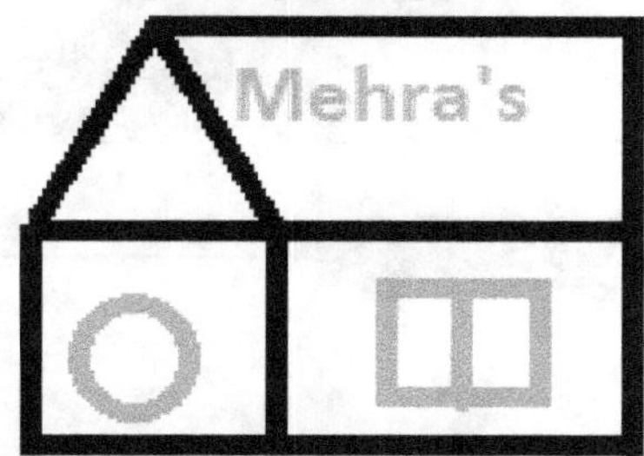

(A) △

(B) ◯

(C) 

(D) ╲

17. What would be the result of the given steps?

Step 1: Select an Oval tool.

Step 2: Go to drawing area, click and drag the mouse to draw an oval shape.

Step 3: Select ◇.

Step 4: Select any colour from the colour palette.

Step 5: Go to the oval shape, and right click the mouse.

(A) ⬭

(B) ⬬

(C) ▭

(D) ▬

18. Which of the following tools is/are used when you want to do the given tasks while drawing?

(1) To draw a rectangle shape.

(2) To use eraser if you make a mistake.

(3) To fill the shape with colour.

(A) ◇

(B) ✐

(C) ▢

(D) All of these

19. The given option is used to ____________ .

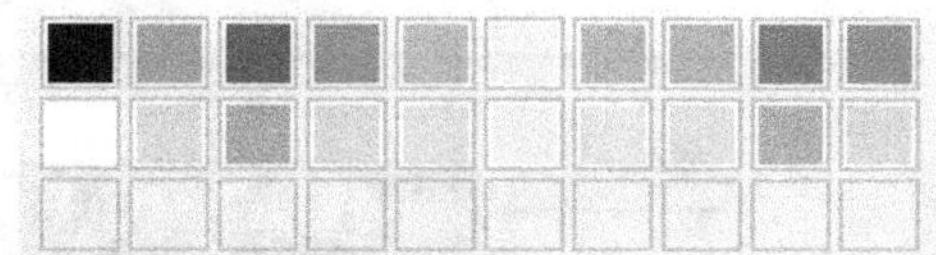

(A) Choose colour for your drawing

(B) Choose shape for your drawing

(C) Choose different tools for your drawing

(D) None of these

20. Identify the following:

■ You can use it to draw free-hand drawing.

■ By using this tool, you can even draw perfect straight line, while holding the key.

(A) ▱

(B) ✐

(C) ⬙

(D) 🔍

1.	Ⓐ Ⓑ Ⓒ Ⓓ	5.	Ⓐ Ⓑ Ⓒ Ⓓ	9.	Ⓐ Ⓑ Ⓒ Ⓓ	13.	Ⓐ Ⓑ Ⓒ Ⓓ	17.	Ⓐ Ⓑ Ⓒ Ⓓ
2.	Ⓐ Ⓑ Ⓒ Ⓓ	6.	Ⓐ Ⓑ Ⓒ Ⓓ	10.	Ⓐ Ⓑ Ⓒ Ⓓ	14.	Ⓐ Ⓑ Ⓒ Ⓓ	18.	Ⓐ Ⓑ Ⓒ Ⓓ
3.	Ⓐ Ⓑ Ⓒ Ⓓ	7.	Ⓐ Ⓑ Ⓒ Ⓓ	11.	Ⓐ Ⓑ Ⓒ Ⓓ	15.	Ⓐ Ⓑ Ⓒ Ⓓ	19.	Ⓐ Ⓑ Ⓒ Ⓓ
4.	Ⓐ Ⓑ Ⓒ Ⓓ	8.	Ⓐ Ⓑ Ⓒ Ⓓ	12.	Ⓐ Ⓑ Ⓒ Ⓓ	16.	Ⓐ Ⓑ Ⓒ Ⓓ	20.	Ⓐ Ⓑ Ⓒ Ⓓ

LATEST DEVELOPMENTS IN 'IT' 

8

➤ Latest developments in the field of IT

MULTIPLE CHOICE QUESTIONS

1. Identify the given device.
   - You can carry it wherever you go as they are small in size and can fit in your pockets.
   - It has a touchscreen as its display screen.
   (A) Laptop
   (B) Desktop computer
   (C) Smartphones
   (D) None of these

2. You can use a smartphone with the help of __________ technology. It allows you to interact with the smartphone with your fingers.
   (A) Touchscreen   (B) Pickscreen
   (C) Dualscreen   (D) Interscreen

3. Which of the following devices comes with touchscreen technology?

   (A)    (B) 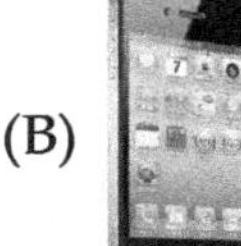

   (C)    (D) Both (A) and (B)

4. Which of the following games can be played on a smartphone?

   (A)    (B) 

   (C)    (D) All of these

5. Identify the given game that can be played on a smartphone or tablet.

   (A) Cut the rope
   (B) Water: Ocean for Kids
   (C) Duck Duck Moose
   (D) Endless Alphabet

6. What do you mean by the term 'App'?
   (A) It is a small program that is found in your mobile device.
   (B) It is a program that erases other programs in a mobile device.

(C) It is a program that is not found on smartphones.

(D) None of these

7. App stands for _______________.
   (A) Application   (B) Applicate
   (C) Applicant   (D) Apply

8. Which of the following is an app?

(A)    (B) 

(C) 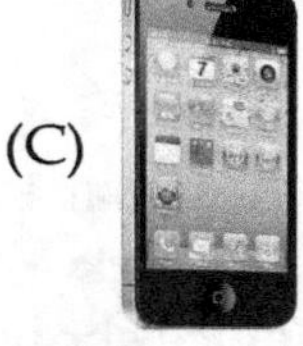   (D) All of these

9. Wearable computers are the devices that can do all the tasks performed by a _______________. You can wear them on the body.
   (A) Smartphone   (B) App
   (C) Application   (D) None of these

10. Which of the following is a wearable computer?

(A)    (B) 

(C) 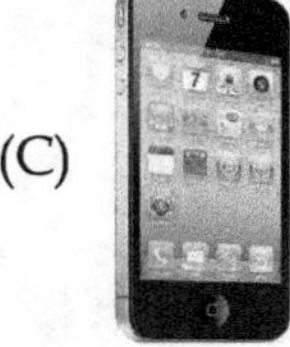   (D) Both (A) and (B)

11. Identify the following:

■ It is a watch that you can wear on your wrist.

■ It can perform all the tasks done by a smartphone.

   (A) Smartwatch   (B) Smartwrist
   (C) Intelligent-wrist   (D) Smarthand

12. Which of the following tasks can be done by a smartwatch?
   (A) Listen to songs   (B) Play games
   (C) Solve sums   (D) All of these

13. Which of the following is an electronic device that is used to play video games and is known as video game console?

(A)    (B) 

(C)    (D) None of these

14. In which of the following devices you can run apps?

(A) 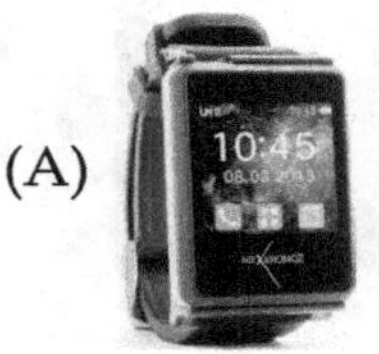   (B) 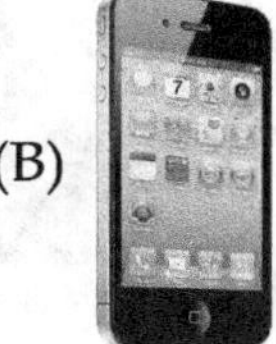

(C)    (D) Both (A) and (B)

15. Which of the following is a gaming device?

(A)    (B) 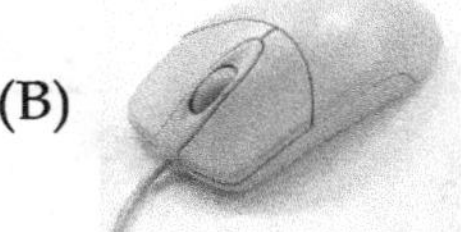

(C)    (D) All of these

16. One terabyte (1 TB) is equal to:
    (A) 1024 GB   (B) 1028 GB
    (C) 1012 GB   (D) 1000 GB

17. This is an image of which operating system version on Android?

    (A) Lollipop   (B) Jellybean
    (C) Kitkat   (D) Cupcake

18. This is an image of which operating system version on Android?

    (A) Donut   (B) Cupcake
    (C) Kitkat   (D) Honeycomb

19. What is the name of this object shown above?

    (A) Mouse   (B) Keyboard
    (C) Gamepad   (D) Joystick

20. What is the name of this device shown in the figure?

    (A) Gamepad   (B) Keyboard
    (C) MICR   (D) CRT

—Darken Your Choice with HB Pencil—

1.	Ⓐ Ⓑ Ⓒ Ⓓ	5.	Ⓐ Ⓑ Ⓒ Ⓓ	9.	Ⓐ Ⓑ Ⓒ Ⓓ	13.	Ⓐ Ⓑ Ⓒ Ⓓ	17.	Ⓐ Ⓑ Ⓒ Ⓓ
2.	Ⓐ Ⓑ Ⓒ Ⓓ	6.	Ⓐ Ⓑ Ⓒ Ⓓ	10.	Ⓐ Ⓑ Ⓒ Ⓓ	14.	Ⓐ Ⓑ Ⓒ Ⓓ	18.	Ⓐ Ⓑ Ⓒ Ⓓ
3.	Ⓐ Ⓑ Ⓒ Ⓓ	7.	Ⓐ Ⓑ Ⓒ Ⓓ	11.	Ⓐ Ⓑ Ⓒ Ⓓ	15.	Ⓐ Ⓑ Ⓒ Ⓓ	19.	Ⓐ Ⓑ Ⓒ Ⓓ
4.	Ⓐ Ⓑ Ⓒ Ⓓ	8.	Ⓐ Ⓑ Ⓒ Ⓓ	12.	Ⓐ Ⓑ Ⓒ Ⓓ	16.	Ⓐ Ⓑ Ⓒ Ⓓ	20.	Ⓐ Ⓑ Ⓒ Ⓓ

LOGICAL REASONING

LEARNING OBJECTIVES

- ➤ Picture-Based Analogy
- ➤ Number-Based Odd One Out
- ➤ Steps to Find Ranking
- ➤ Concepts of Measurement
- ➤ Types of Patterns
- ➤ Concepts of Spatial Understanding

MULTIPLE CHOICE QUESTIONS

Direction (Qs. 1–3): Find the matching pair.

1.  :  ::  : **?**

(A)  (B) 

(C)  (D) 

2.   :  ::  : **?**

(A)  (B) 

(C)  (D) 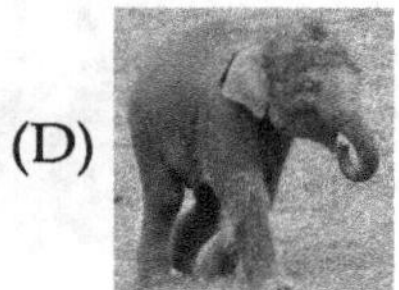

3.  :  ::

 : **?**

(A) 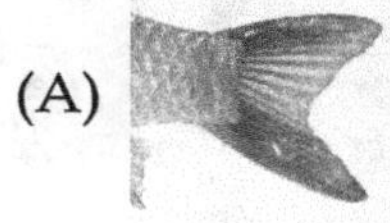 (B) 

(C)  (D) 

Direction: Find the odd one out.

4.

(A) 

(B) 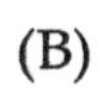 

(C) 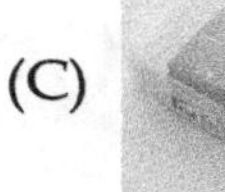  (D) 

5.

(A) 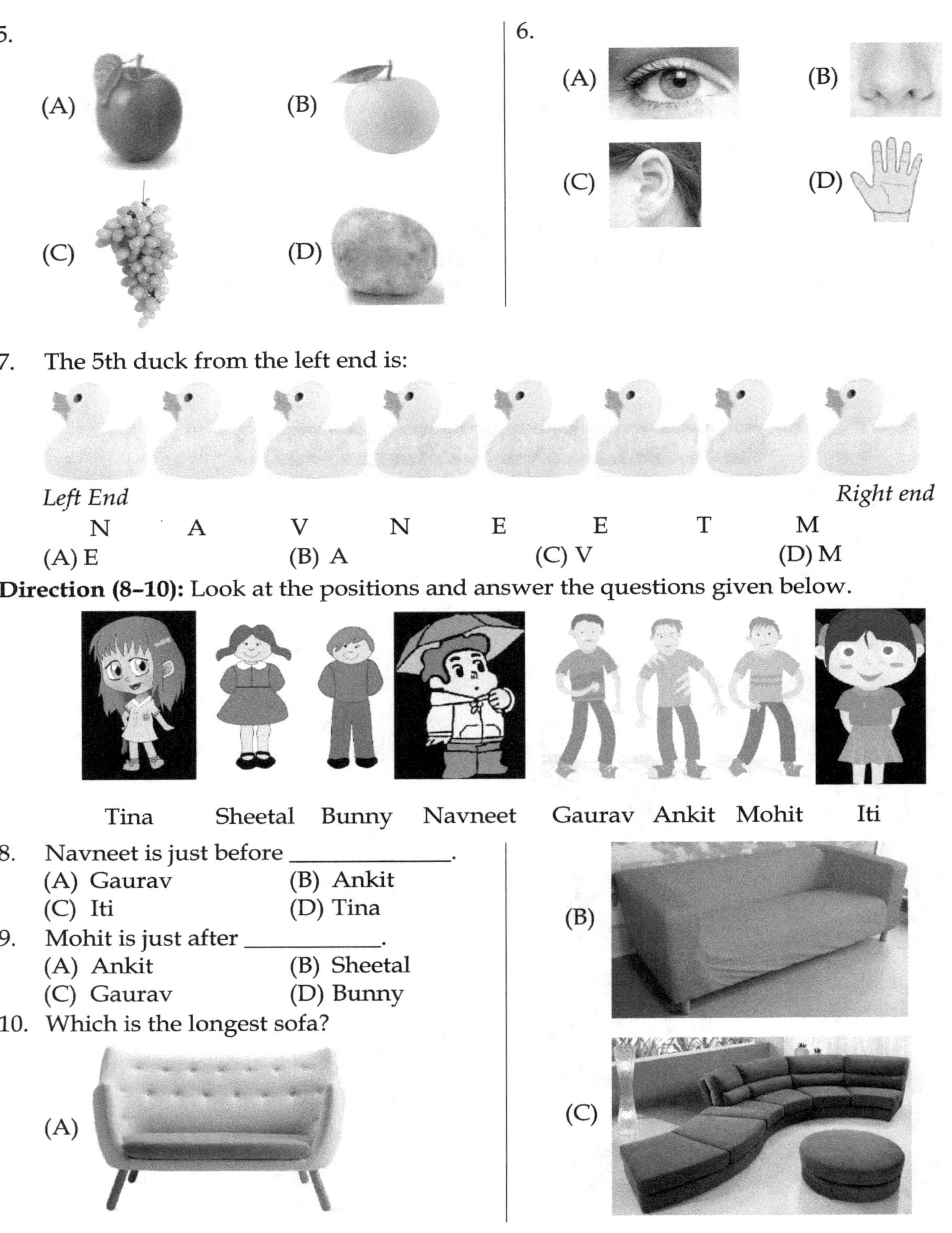

(B)

(C)

(D)

6.

(A)   (B)

(C)   (D)

7. The 5th duck from the left end is:

Left End   *Right end*

    N   A   V   N   E   E   T   M

(A) E   (B) A   (C) V   (D) M

Direction (8–10): Look at the positions and answer the questions given below.

    Tina   Sheetal Bunny Navneet Gaurav Ankit Mohit   Iti

8. Navneet is just before ______________.
    (A) Gaurav   (B) Ankit
    (C) Iti   (D) Tina

9. Mohit is just after ____________.
    (A) Ankit   (B) Sheetal
    (C) Gaurav   (D) Bunny

10. Which is the longest sofa?

(A)

(B)

(C)

(D)

11. Golu's toffee basket has 2 eclairs, 4 chocolates and 4 gems. Golu has one lollipop less than chocolates. How many lollipops are there in Golu's toffee basket?

(A) 3   (B) 2

(C) 5   (D) 4

12. Which scale is smaller than scale B?

(A) 

(B) 

(C) 

(D) 

Direction (13-15): What comes next in the given series?

13.      ?

(A)    (B) 

14.

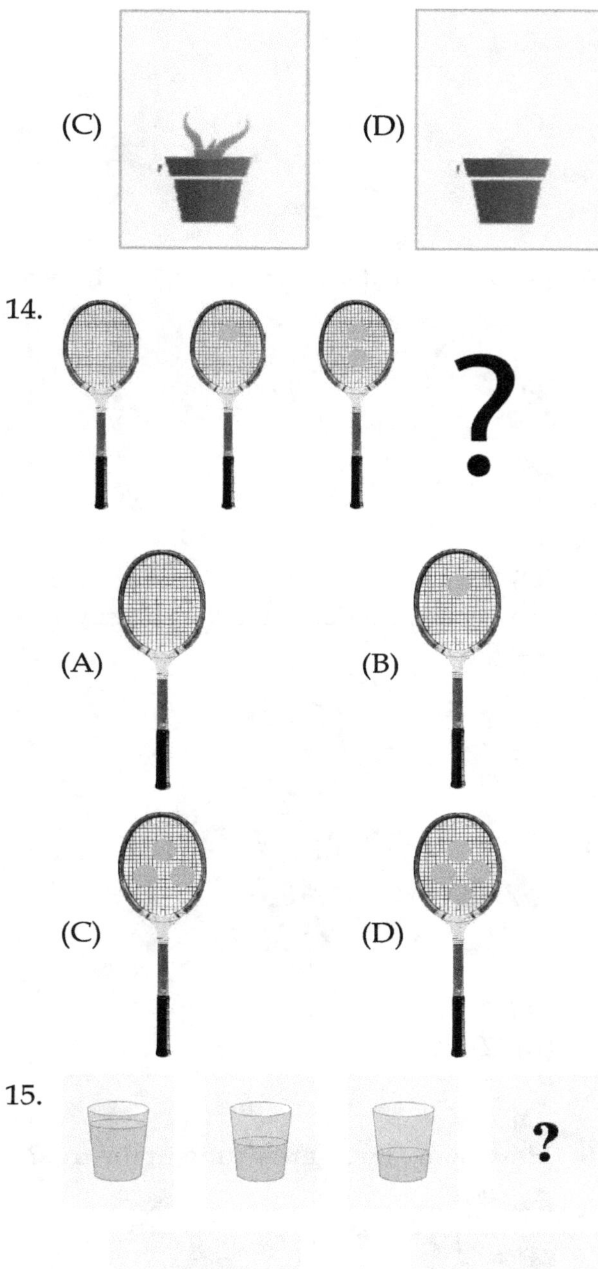

(C)   (D)

(A)   (B)

(C)   (D)

15.  ?

(A) 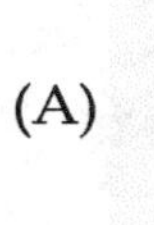    (B) 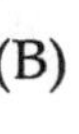 

(C) 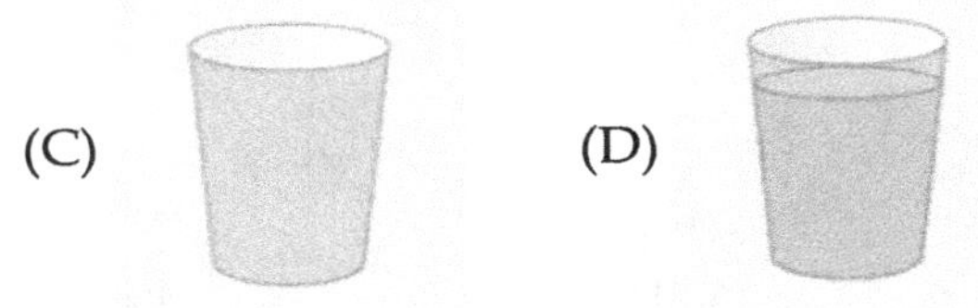 (D)

16. How many balls are there outside the box?

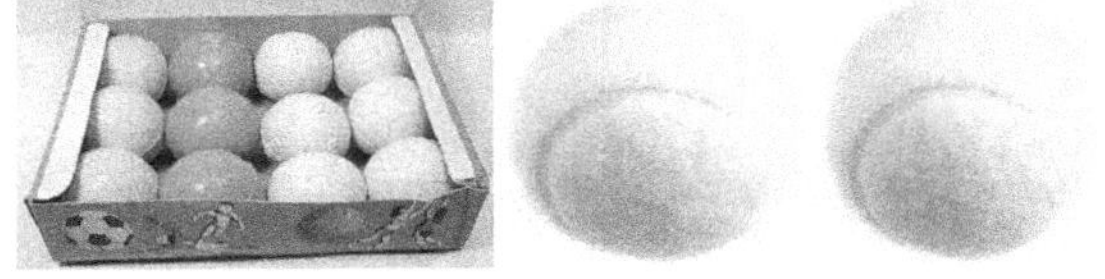

(A) 4
(B) 6
(C) 2
(D) 8

17. How many students are standing outside the bus?

(A) 1
(B) 2
(C) 4
(D) 6

18. How many birds are sitting in the tree?

(A) 4   (B) 5
(C) 8   (D) 6

19. There are ______ squares in the given figure.

(A) 4
(B) 5
(C) 6
(D) 8

20. Which one of the following is a circle?

(A) 

(B)

(C)

(D)

21. Choose the right name of the shape given below?

(A) Circle
(B) Square
(C) Triangle
(D) Rectangle

OLYMPIAD WORKBOOK (NCO) CLASS – 1

22. How many groups of 2's can be formed from the flowers given below?

(A) 8   (B) 9   (C) 10   (D) 12

23. There are ____________ groups of 5 triangles.

(A) 3   (B) 4   (C) 3   (D) 2

24. There are _______ groups of 2 pencils.

(A) 7   (B) 3   (C) 5   (D) 8

1.	Ⓐ Ⓑ Ⓒ Ⓓ	6.	Ⓐ Ⓑ Ⓒ Ⓓ	11.	Ⓐ Ⓑ Ⓒ Ⓓ	16.	Ⓐ Ⓑ Ⓒ Ⓓ	21.	Ⓐ Ⓑ Ⓒ Ⓓ
2.	Ⓐ Ⓑ Ⓒ Ⓓ	7.	Ⓐ Ⓑ Ⓒ Ⓓ	12.	Ⓐ Ⓑ Ⓒ Ⓓ	17.	Ⓐ Ⓑ Ⓒ Ⓓ	22.	Ⓐ Ⓑ Ⓒ Ⓓ
3.	Ⓐ Ⓑ Ⓒ Ⓓ	8.	Ⓐ Ⓑ Ⓒ Ⓓ	13.	Ⓐ Ⓑ Ⓒ Ⓓ	18.	Ⓐ Ⓑ Ⓒ Ⓓ	23.	Ⓐ Ⓑ Ⓒ Ⓓ
4.	Ⓐ Ⓑ Ⓒ Ⓓ	9.	Ⓐ Ⓑ Ⓒ Ⓓ	14.	Ⓐ Ⓑ Ⓒ Ⓓ	19.	Ⓐ Ⓑ Ⓒ Ⓓ	24.	Ⓐ Ⓑ Ⓒ Ⓓ
5.	Ⓐ Ⓑ Ⓒ Ⓓ	10.	Ⓐ Ⓑ Ⓒ Ⓓ	15.	Ⓐ Ⓑ Ⓒ Ⓓ	20.	Ⓐ Ⓑ Ⓒ Ⓓ		

MODEL TEST PAPER

MULTIPLE CHOICE QUESTIONS

1. If all the As and T's are dropped from the arrangement given below, which of the following will be the fifth from the left end of the new arrangement?

   N A V N E E T M E H R A

   (A) E
   (B) R
   (C) C
   (D) S

2. In a row there are six students standing and waiting for the bus. If we interchange the 3rd one with the 2nd, what will be the rank of the 3rd student from left in the newly formed sequence?

   (A) 2
   (B) 3
   (C) 4
   (D) 5

3. Observe the picture and tell which of the following statements is correct?

   (A) Golu is as heavy as Ankit
   (B) Golu is lighter than Ankit
   (C) Golu is heavier than Ankit
   (D) None of these

4. There are _____ mangoes in each group.

   (A) 8
   (B) 9
   (C) 5
   (D) 4

5. Estimate the weight of the book.

   (A) 1.5 kg
   (B) 25 kg
   (C) 3 gm
   (D) 9 gm

6. Sinha has a DVD of a new movie. He wants to watch this movie. Is it possible for him to watch the movie on the computer?

   (A) Yes
   (B) No
   (C) Possibility is less
   (D) Possibility is more

7. What is the name of this object shown above?

   (A) Mouse
   (B) Keyboard
   (C) Gamepad
   (D) Joystick

OLYMPIAD WORKBOOK (NCO) CLASS — 1

8. What is the name of this device shown in the figure?

(A) Gamepad   (B) Keyboard
(C) MICR   (D) CRT

9. Identify the following:
   - It can be wirelessly connected to the computer.
   - It is used to enter letters and numbers into the computer.

(A)    (B) 

(C)    (D) 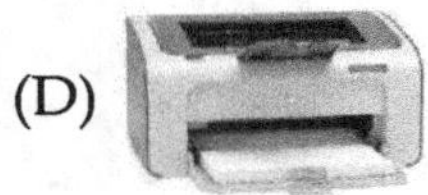

10. Match the following:

Column-I		Column-II
a		1	Used to watch movies
b		2	Known as brain of a computer
c		3	Used to type letters into the computer

(A) a-2, b-3, c-1
(B) a-1, b-2, c-3
(C) a-2, b-1, c-3
(D) a-1, b-3, c-2

11. One terabyte (1 TB) is equal to:
(A) 1024 GB   (B) 1028 GB
(C) 1012 GB   (D) 1000 GB

12. This is an image of which operating system version on Android?

(A) Lollipop   (B) Jellybean
(C) Kitkat   (D) Cupcake

13. Select the CORRECT statement about the given jumbled word.

MUOES

(A) It is used for pointing items on computer screen.
(B) It is used to enter letters on computer.
(C) It is used to listen to music.
(D) It controls all the working of computer.

14. This is an image of which operating system version on Android?

(A) Donut   (B) Cupcake
(C) Kitkat   (D) Honeycomb

15. You want to do the following tasks:

To type letters in a computer.

To create a copy of those letters onto the sheet of paper.

Which of the following parts of computer is/ are needed?
(A) Keyboard   (B) Printer
(C) Speakers   (D) Both (A) and (B)

16. Solving the sums on computers is ______.
(A) Easy and time-consuming
(B) Difficult and time-consuming
(C) Easy and fast
(D) Difficult and fast

17. _______ key is also called as return key.
    (A) Space bar   (B) Enter
    (C) Delete   (D) Backspace

18. The keys from 0 to 9 are called _____ keys.
    (A) Alphabet   (B) Arrow
    (C) Number   (D) Special

19. Which of the following statements is CORRECT about mouse?
    (A) It is hand-operated device.
    (B) It sits outside the computer case.
    (C) It comes in many shapes and sizes.
    (D) All of these

20. Which of the following is the longest key on the keyboard?
    (A) Delete   (B) Spacebar
    (C) Enter   (D) Ctrl

21. Using computer keyboard, you can do ___________.
    (A) Typing   (B) Clicking
    (C) Hitting   (D) Pushing

22. A computer is a machine which helps us to _______.
    (A) Play games
    (B) Watch movies
    (C) Listen to music
    (D) All of these

23. Which of the following statements is CORRECT with respect to the given icon of MS-Paint in Windows 10?

    (A) It can be used as a Color Picker tool.
    (B) It is known as Crayon brush.
    (C) It is found under View tab.
    (D) We can change its width while coloring the picture.

24. What does the arrow on the computer monitor shown in the given image is called?

    (A) Mouse pointer
    (B) Mouse spot
    (C) Mouse track
    (D) Mouse pad

25. Which of the following portions of start menu will you click to shut down the computer?

    (A) P   (B) Q
    (C) R   (D) S

26. To start a laptop, you just need to ______.
    (A) Press power button available on the laptop
    (B) Press the ⊞ key
    (C) Tap twice on touchpad
    (D) Press the ⇧ Shift key

27. Which of the following tools has been used in the given image?

OLYMPIAD WORKBOOK (NCO) CLASS— 1

(A) 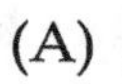   (B) 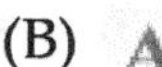

(C)    (D) 

28. Which of the following tools is NOT used while drawing the given picture?

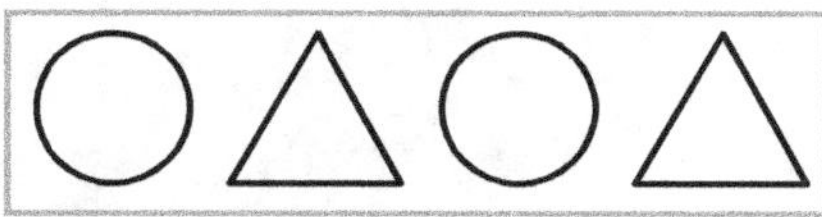

(A) Oval tool   (B) Rectangle tool

(C) Pencil tool   (D) Line tool

29. Which of the following tools help you to draw the free-form lines shown here?

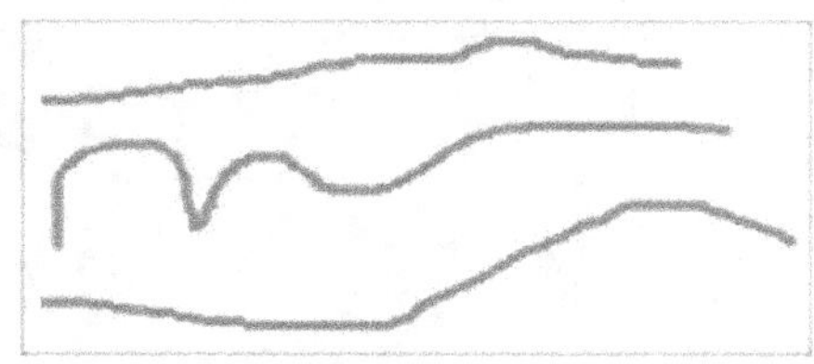

(A)   (B) A

(C)   (D)

30. Which of the following runs on electricity?

(A) 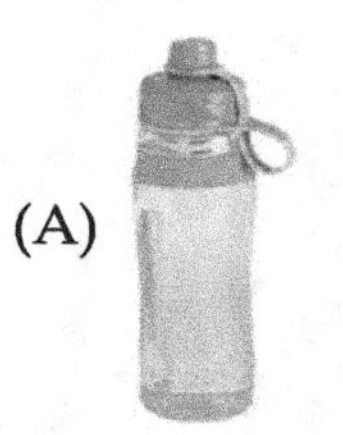   (B) 

(C)    (D) 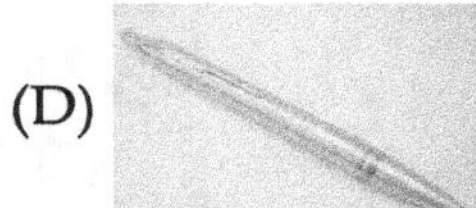

31. Which of the following statements is CORRECT about the given device?

(A) It is a type of computer.

(B) It can be carried from one place to another.

(C) It is called laptop.

(D) All of these

32. Identify the pictures marked as 1 and 2 and select the CORRECT statement.

1   2

(A) 1 – It is a man-made machine and it runs on fuel.
    2 – It is an electronic machine.

(B) 1 – It is made by nature.
    2 – It is not a man-made machine.

(C) 1 – It is not a man-made machine.
    2 – It is an electronic machine.

(D) 1 – It is an electronic machine.
    2 – It is made by nature.

33. Select the INCORRECT match regarding the uses of computer.

(A) Offices – Maintaining employee records

(B) Schools – Diagnosing diseases

(C) Banks – Money withdrawal through ATM

(D) Railways – Booking Tickets

34. Select the word which when unscrambled gives the name of a place where computers are used.

(A) SMUS   (B) VOLSE

(C) NABK   (D) POME

35. Which of the following statements is INCORRECT about alphabet keys?

(A) They are used for typing letters and words.

(B) There are 26 alphabet keys on the keyboard.

(C) The first six letters of alphabet keys form the name of a keyboard layout.

(D) The last seven letters of the alphabet keys form the name of the inventor of keyboard.

1.	Ⓐ Ⓑ Ⓒ Ⓓ	8.	Ⓐ Ⓑ Ⓒ Ⓓ	15.	Ⓐ Ⓑ Ⓒ Ⓓ	22.	Ⓐ Ⓑ Ⓒ Ⓓ	29.	Ⓐ Ⓑ Ⓒ Ⓓ
2.	Ⓐ Ⓑ Ⓒ Ⓓ	9.	Ⓐ Ⓑ Ⓒ Ⓓ	16.	Ⓐ Ⓑ Ⓒ Ⓓ	23.	Ⓐ Ⓑ Ⓒ Ⓓ	30.	Ⓐ Ⓑ Ⓒ Ⓓ
3.	Ⓐ Ⓑ Ⓒ Ⓓ	10.	Ⓐ Ⓑ Ⓒ Ⓓ	17.	Ⓐ Ⓑ Ⓒ Ⓓ	24.	Ⓐ Ⓑ Ⓒ Ⓓ	31.	Ⓐ Ⓑ Ⓒ Ⓓ
4.	Ⓐ Ⓑ Ⓒ Ⓓ	11.	Ⓐ Ⓑ Ⓒ Ⓓ	18.	Ⓐ Ⓑ Ⓒ Ⓓ	25.	Ⓐ Ⓑ Ⓒ Ⓓ	32.	Ⓐ Ⓑ Ⓒ Ⓓ
5.	Ⓐ Ⓑ Ⓒ Ⓓ	12.	Ⓐ Ⓑ Ⓒ Ⓓ	19.	Ⓐ Ⓑ Ⓒ Ⓓ	26.	Ⓐ Ⓑ Ⓒ Ⓓ	33.	Ⓐ Ⓑ Ⓒ Ⓓ
6.	Ⓐ Ⓑ Ⓒ Ⓓ	13.	Ⓐ Ⓑ Ⓒ Ⓓ	20.	Ⓐ Ⓑ Ⓒ Ⓓ	27.	Ⓐ Ⓑ Ⓒ Ⓓ	34.	Ⓐ Ⓑ Ⓒ Ⓓ
7.	Ⓐ Ⓑ Ⓒ Ⓓ	14.	Ⓐ Ⓑ Ⓒ Ⓓ	21.	Ⓐ Ⓑ Ⓒ Ⓓ	28.	Ⓐ Ⓑ Ⓒ Ⓓ	35.	Ⓐ Ⓑ Ⓒ Ⓓ

OLYMPIAD WORKBOOK (NCO) CLASS— 1

HINTS AND SOLUTIONS

1. INTRODUCTION TO COMPUTER

Answer Key

1. (D)	2. (C)	3. (B)	4. (C)	5. (A)	6. (D)	7. (A)	8. (D)	9. (A)	10. (D)
11. (A)	12. (A)	13. (A)	14. (B)	15. (A)					

1. (D)

Option (a) shows Juicer, Option (b) shows Laptop, Option (c) shows Digicam, and, Option (d) shows Dog. Dogs are not man-made machines, and Options (a), (b) and (c) are machines made by humans.

3. (B)

Option (b) shows laptop where you can play songs.

5. (A)

Picture marked as '1' shows Desktop computer, Picture marked as '2' shows laptop, Picture marked as '3' shows mobile phone. Desktop computer needs large amount of space on table than laptop. Laptop can easily fit in your lap. Mobile phone can be carried in our pockets.

10. (D)

Picture marked as '1' shows washing machine, Picture marked as '2' shows Scooty and Picture marked as '3' shows mobile. All are man-made and electronic machines.

12. (A)

By arranging the jumbled letters in correct manner, you will get the word: COMPUTER.

14. (B)

Name of the pictures from left to right is as follows:

Table	Apple	Ball	Lamp	Elephant	Tortoise
T	A	B	L	E	T

By using the first letter of these words, the word 'TABLET' is formed.

15. (A)

COMPUTER is the name of machine hidden in the given grid.

HOTS (ACHIEVERS SECTION)

16. (D)	17. (A)	18. (D)	19. (A)	20. (D)

17. (A)

Picture marked as 1 shows train and picture marked as 2 shows computer. Car is a man-made machine and it runs on fuel. Computer is an electronic machine.

Answer Key

1. (D)	2. (A)	3. (D)	4. (A)	5. (B)	6. (D)	7. (A)	8. (D)	9. (D)	10. (A)
11. (B)	12. (D)	13. (D)	14. (D)	15. (A)	16. (B)	17. (B)	18. (B)	19. (A)	20. (A)

1. (D)
   Option (a) shows CPU, Option (b) shows a mouse, Option (c) shows a monitor and Option (d) shows a lamp. So, (a), (b) and (c) are parts of a computer.

2. (A)
   Monitor is a display screen that is used to watch movies on a computer.

3. (D)
   Both mouse and keyboard can be wired or wireless.

4. (A)
   Option (a) shows mouse. So, it is an incorrect match.

6. (D)
   Given device shows CPU, which is known as brain of a computer. It controls all the workings of a computer.

7. (A)
   Speakers are used to listen songs.

11. (B)
    Without a CPU, a computer cannot work.

13. (D)
    Printer is used to copy the computer screen onto a sheet of paper.

14. (D)
    When you arrange the jumbled letters in correct form, the word MONITOR is formed.

17. (B)
    The two words Mouse and CPU are hidden in the given grid.

18. (B)
    Option (b) shows keyboard. It is used to enter numbers, alphabets and words into a computer.

19. (A)
    When the given jumbled letters are arranged in correct manner, it will form a word: MOUSE.

HOTS (ACHIEVERS SECTION)

21. (A)	22. (B)	23. (B)	24. (A)	25. (A)

22. (B)
    The two words MOUSE and CPU are hidden in the given grid.

23. (B)
    Option [B] is of keyboard. It is used to enter numbers, alphabets and words into a computer.

24. (A)
    When the given jumbled word is arranged in correct manner, it will form a word: MOUSE.

3. USES OF COMPUTER

Answer Key

1. (D)	2. (D)	3. (C)	4. (A)	5. (D)	6. (C)	7. (C)	8. (C)	9. (D)	10. (B)
11. (D)	12. (D)	13. (B)	14. (D)	15. (D)					

1. **(D)**
   In option (d), a player is playing cricket without using computer.
3. **(C)**
   Pencil and paper are used in a drawing book.
6. **(C)**
   Only games are played for entertainment. So, option (c) is correct.
7. **(D)**
   Computers make calculations easy and very fast.
12. **(D)**
   In banks, computers are used for banking operations such as to deposit money, to withdraw money, etc.
13. **(B)**
   Only laptop can be used while travelling as it is easy to carry.
15. **(D)**
   We do not watch music, we listen to it, so (a) and (b) are correct.

HOTS (ACHIEVERS SECTION)

16. (B)	17. (B)	18. (C)	19. (D)	20. (A)

16. **(B)**
   Activities hidden in the given grid are: Drawing, Playing and Typing.

```
V  A  X  U  S  D  E  R
D  P  L  A  Y  I  N  G
R  C  V  T  H  F  S  C
A  S  A  Y  M  R  V  B
W  O  F  P  I  C  E  R
I  T  B  I  F  I  K  L
N  O  A  N  N  K  A  N
G  N  L  G  A  T  I  O
```

18. **(C)**
   Unscrambled words are: (a) Sums, (b) Solve, (c) Bank and (d) Poem. Out of these, bank is a place where computers are used.
19. **(D)**
   At departmental stores, computers are used to keep details of items sold and to print bills.
20. **(A)**
   You cannot draw pictures as shown in other options.

4. KEYBOARD AND ITS KEYS

Answer Key

1. (D)	2. (B)	3. (C)	4. (D)	5. (D)	6. (D)	7. (C)	8. (C)	9. (B)	10. (D)
11. (D)	12. (D)	13. (B)	14. (A)	15. (C)					

1. **(D)**
   Pen and pencil are used to write on a paper, and printer is used to take print-outs. Only keyboard is used to type letters.
3. **(C)**
   The keys from A to Z are alphabet keys.
4. **(D)**
   It is a number key, not an alphabet key. Pressing it once will type a 0 (zero).
6. **(D)**
   The Shift Key does not bring the cursor to right.

8. (C)
Key is used in combination with the number keys to type symbols printed on them. It is also used to type in capital letters when caps lock is off and to type in lower case letters when capslock is on.

10. (D)
As there are no L and T keys to form the word Delete, so option (D) is the correct answer.

HOTS (ACHIEVERS SECTION)

16. (D)	17. (C)	18. (B)	19. (C)	20. (D)

16. (D)
After pressing the key two times, the cursor is after the letter R.

R | IGHT Cursor

Pressing the Backspace key deletes the letter R.

Pressing the T key types T at cursor position.

19. (C)
The words Delete, number and alphabet are hidden in the given grid as shown here.

U	N	I	L	O	P	F	D	S	X
N	O	L	A	D	E	L	E	T	E
R	B	T	I	K	S	L	E	W	V
A	L	W	N	U	M	B	E	R	T
Z	B	A	C	K	B	E	T	P	A
T	A	L	P	H	A	B	E	T	R
R	V	S	M	D	G	A	I	E	D

5. COMPUTER MOUSE

Answer Key

1. (D)	2. (A)	3. (A)	4. (C)	5. (A)	6. (B)	7. (B)	8. (B)	9. (A)	10. (A)
11. (D)	12. (B)	13. (C)	14. (D)	15. (D)					

3. (A)
It is connected to the CPU because the CPU makes all the parts of a computer work.

4. (C)
The wheel shown at the centre of the given image is the scroll wheel of mouse.

10. (A)
When we right-click on an object, a short menu is displayed about the tasks that can be performed.

12. (B)
Wireless means without a wire (cable). So, option (b) is correct answer.

13. (C)
We can see in the image that the left mouse button is clicked.

HOTS (ACHIEVERS SECTION)

16. (D)	17. (C)	18. (C)	19. (D)	20. (B)

16. (D)

Unscrambled words are monitor, printer, mouse and pointer. Out of these, only option (D) completes the sentence correctly.

17. (C)

The hidden words are twiggle, scroll and click.

T	W	I	G	G	L	E
A	S	L	M	O	R	M
N	X	C	L	I	C	K
S	F	I	T	W	R	A
M	S	C	R	O	L	L
I	P	A	C	K	B	U
R	T	T	O	N	T	A

19. (D)

Computer mouse does not eat grain. It helps to draw and it is controlled by hand.

6. STARTING AND SHUTTING DOWN A COMPUTER

Answer Key

1. (A)	2. (B)	3. (D)	4. (A)	5. (A)	6. (B)	7. (D)	8. (C)	9. (A)	10. (A)
11. (C)	12. (C)	13. (A)	14. (B)	15. (C)					

2. (B)

The screen with icons, taskbar and start button is called a desktop.

4. (A)

Monitor is switched on by pressing the power button on it.

5. (A)

We use a mouse to click on the shut down option.

6. (B)

We should never sit too close to the monitor. The eatables should be kept away. We should use the keyboard very gently. We should not play with any wires. So, only option (b) is correct.

10. (A)

It is covered to keep the dust away from it.

13. (A)

As laptop is an all-in-one computer, it has a CPU, a monitor, a keyboard built into one machine. So, we need not switch on each part separately. We just need to press the power button on it.

15. (C)

The unscrambled word is BOOTING, it is performed when CPU is turned on.

HOTS (ACHIEVERS SECTION)

16. (C)	17. (D)	18. (B)	19. (A)	20. (C)

19. (A)

The name assigned to a user to access a computer is called username, the secret combination of alphabets and numbers is called password.

20. (C)

Monitor is powered on in the end, while starting a computer.

7. INTRODUCTION TO MS-PAINT

Answer Key

1. (A)	2. (A)	3. (B)	4. (D)	5. (C)	6. (C)	7. (D)	8. (A)	9. (A)	10. (A)
11. (A)	12. (A)	13. (C)	14. (D)	15. (D)					

2. (A)

In the given image, free-hand drawing is shown. Pencil tool is used for free hand drawing.

3. (B)

Some parts of the image in Picture 2 have been erased with the help of the Eraser tool.

4. (D)

There is no line tool.

5. (C)

Option (A) shows Eraser tool. It is used to erase your drawing if you made a mistake. Option (B) shows Rectangle tool, it is used to draw rectangle shape. Option (C) shows Line tool, it is used to draw straight lines. Option (D) shows Oval tool, it is used to draw circles. So, option (C) is CORRECT.

6. (C)

In the given picture, no free-hand shapes are shown. Pencil tool is used to draw free-hand drawing.

7. (D)

In MS-Paint, Ribbon is the area where different tools are used for drawing purpose.

8. (A)

The given tool shows 'Fill with Color'.

10. (A)

Option (A) shows 'Fill with Color' tool, it is used to fill the shape with colour. It is not used to draw shapes.

14. (D)

Line tool is used to draw straight lines.

15. (D)

Closed shape means the shape in which no area is left open. Option (A) shows the Rectangle tool and option (B) shows the Oval tool. Both are used to draw closed shapes only.

HOTS (ACHIEVERS SECTION)

16. (C)	17. (B)	18. (D)	19. (A)	20. (B)

16. (C)

The tools used in the given image are: Line tool, Rectangle tool and Oval tool. Option (C) shows 'Fill with Colour' tool, that is not used in the given drawing. It is used to fill the drawing with colours, and no colours or shading is shown in the given drawing.

8. LATEST DEVELOPMENTS IN 'IT'

Answer Key

1. (C)	2. (A)	3. (D)	4. (D)	5. (A)	6. (A)	7. (A)	8. (A)	9. (A)	10. (D)
11. (A)	12. (D)	13. (A)	14. (D)	15. (A)					

1. (C)
The given description is of a smartphone. This phone is called smart because it combines the features of a personal computer with other features useful for a mobile device.

3. (D)
Option (A) shows smartphone, and option (B) shows tablet. Both come with touchscreen technology. Option (c) shows Desktop Computer you can interact with it with the help of keyboard and mouse.

4. (D)
Option (A) shows Candy Crush Saga, option (B) shows Super Mario and option (C) shows Angry Birds. All of them are the games that can be played on a smartphone.

8. (A)
App is a program found in the smartphone. Option (A) shows Drawing app, which is found in a smartphone. Option (B) shows smartphone and option (C) shows tablet computer. Both (B) and (C) are devices not apps.

10. (D)
Option (a) shows smartwatch and option (b) shows Google Glasses. They both are wearable computers. And option (C) shows smartphone that you can carry in your pockets. It is not a wearable device.

HOTS (ACHIEVERS SECTION)

16. (A)	17. (D)	18. (C)	19. (D)	20. (C)

9. LOGICAL REASONING

Answer Key

1. (B)	2. (A)	3. (A)	4. (D)	5. (D)	6. (D)	7. (A)	8. (A)	9. (A)	10. (C)
11. (A)	12. (D)	13. (B)	14. (C)	15. (C)	16. (C)	17. (B)	18. (D)	19. (C)	20. (B)
21. (D)	22. (B)	23. (B)	24. (C)						

1. (B)
Umbrella is used when it's raining.

2. (D)
Potato is not a fruit but all other options are.

3. (D)
Hand is not a part of the face.

4. (C)
Sofa C is longest among them.

5. (A)
There are 3 lollipops in Golu's toffee basket.

6. (D)
Scale D is smaller than scale B.

7. (C)
Racket with three balls will be next one.

MODEL TEST PAPER

Answer Key

1. (A)	2. (A)	3. (C)	4. (D)	5. (A)	6. (A)	7. (D)	8. (C)	9. (B)	10. (A)
11. (A)	12. (D)	13. (A)	14. (C)	15. (D)	16. (C)	17. (B)	18. (C)	19. (D)	20. (B)
21. (A)	22. (D)	23. (A)	24. (A)	25. (D)	26. (A)	27. (A)	28. (C)	29. (A)	30. (C)
31. (D)	32. (A)	33. (B)	34. (C)	35. (D)					

HINTS AND SOLUTIONS

SAMPLE OMR ANSWER SHEET

1. STUDENT NAME (IN ENGLISH CAPITAL LETTERS ONLY)

Students must write and darken the respective circles completely using HB Pencil only. Othewise their Answer Sheets will not be evaluated.

PERSONAL DETAILS

2. SCHOOL CODE

3. CLASS

4. SECTION

5. ROLL NO.

6. QUESTION PAPER SET

A ◯   B ◯   C ◯   D ◯

7. MOBILE NUMBER

8. GENDER

MALE ◯

FEMALE ◯

9. STREAM
(Only for Class XI and XII Students)

MATHEMATICS ◯
BIOLOGY ◯
OTHERS ◯

MARK YOUR ANSWERS

1. Ⓐ Ⓑ Ⓒ Ⓓ	26. Ⓐ Ⓑ Ⓒ Ⓓ
2. Ⓐ Ⓑ Ⓒ Ⓓ	27. Ⓐ Ⓑ Ⓒ Ⓓ
3. Ⓐ Ⓑ Ⓒ Ⓓ	28. Ⓐ Ⓑ Ⓒ Ⓓ
4. Ⓐ Ⓑ Ⓒ Ⓓ	29. Ⓐ Ⓑ Ⓒ Ⓓ
5. Ⓐ Ⓑ Ⓒ Ⓓ	30. Ⓐ Ⓑ Ⓒ Ⓓ
6. Ⓐ Ⓑ Ⓒ Ⓓ	31. Ⓐ Ⓑ Ⓒ Ⓓ
7. Ⓐ Ⓑ Ⓒ Ⓓ	32. Ⓐ Ⓑ Ⓒ Ⓓ
8. Ⓐ Ⓑ Ⓒ Ⓓ	33. Ⓐ Ⓑ Ⓒ Ⓓ
9. Ⓐ Ⓑ Ⓒ Ⓓ	34. Ⓐ Ⓑ Ⓒ Ⓓ
10. Ⓐ Ⓑ Ⓒ Ⓓ	35. Ⓐ Ⓑ Ⓒ Ⓓ
11. Ⓐ Ⓑ Ⓒ Ⓓ	36. Ⓐ Ⓑ Ⓒ Ⓓ
12. Ⓐ Ⓑ Ⓒ Ⓓ	37. Ⓐ Ⓑ Ⓒ Ⓓ
13. Ⓐ Ⓑ Ⓒ Ⓓ	38. Ⓐ Ⓑ Ⓒ Ⓓ
14. Ⓐ Ⓑ Ⓒ Ⓓ	39. Ⓐ Ⓑ Ⓒ Ⓓ
15. Ⓐ Ⓑ Ⓒ Ⓓ	40. Ⓐ Ⓑ Ⓒ Ⓓ
16. Ⓐ Ⓑ Ⓒ Ⓓ	41. Ⓐ Ⓑ Ⓒ Ⓓ
17. Ⓐ Ⓑ Ⓒ Ⓓ	42. Ⓐ Ⓑ Ⓒ Ⓓ
18. Ⓐ Ⓑ Ⓒ Ⓓ	43. Ⓐ Ⓑ Ⓒ Ⓓ
19. Ⓐ Ⓑ Ⓒ Ⓓ	44. Ⓐ Ⓑ Ⓒ Ⓓ
20. Ⓐ Ⓑ Ⓒ Ⓓ	45. Ⓐ Ⓑ Ⓒ Ⓓ
21. Ⓐ Ⓑ Ⓒ Ⓓ	46. Ⓐ Ⓑ Ⓒ Ⓓ
22. Ⓐ Ⓑ Ⓒ Ⓓ	47. Ⓐ Ⓑ Ⓒ Ⓓ
23. Ⓐ Ⓑ Ⓒ Ⓓ	48. Ⓐ Ⓑ Ⓒ Ⓓ
24. Ⓐ Ⓑ Ⓒ Ⓓ	49. Ⓐ Ⓑ Ⓒ Ⓓ
25. Ⓐ Ⓑ Ⓒ Ⓓ	50. Ⓐ Ⓑ Ⓒ Ⓓ

Signature of the Student & Date of Examination

Signature of the Invigilator & Date of Examination